Men With Adult ADHD

2 in 1

The Practical Guide with 90+ CBT, DBT, and Mind Mapping Exercises to Manage Anxiety and Enhance Focus, Resilience, Motivation, and Executive Functioning.

Jimmy Taylor

A SELFTRANSFORMATIONPATH BOOK

Contents

Free Bonus 5

Mind Mapping for Men with Adult ADHD
Book 1

Introduction 8

Part One
The ADHD Brain and Overthinking

1. Understanding ADHD 13
2. Adult ADHD in Men 31
3. Your Thought Spiral 51

Part Two
Self-Regulation for Positive Transformation

4. Your Guide to Mind Mapping 63
5. Executive Functioning 101 81
6. Boosting Your Emotional Quotient (EQ) 100

Part Three
Improved Memory and Functioning

7. The Power of Neuroplasticity 111
8. Thriving With ADHD 131

Conclusion 137
References 139

Men with Adult ADHD Workbook
Book 2

Introduction 144

1. Mind Mapping and Its Application 147

2. Executive Functioning 155

3. Emotional Regulation 167

4. Social Well-Being 178

5. Overthinking and Intrusive Thoughts 191

6. Overwhelm, Fear of Rejection, and Rejection
Sensitivity 204

7. Time Management, Procrastination, and Analysis
Paralysis 216

8. Dealing with ADHD Learning Disabilities and
Comorbid Conditions 229

9. Enhancing Motivation and Self-Discipline 248

10. Creating Healthy Habits for ADHD Symptom
Management 265

11. Improving ADHD Creativity 278

12. Building Resilience and Enhancing Tenacity 293

Conclusion 309

Thank You 311

References 312

Mind Mapping for Men with Adult ADHD

Daily Brain Exercises and Strategies for a Positive Transformation to Control Anxious Thoughts, Improve Concentration, and Productivity

Book 1

Introduction

I grew up believing that attention deficit hyperactivity disorder (ADHD) was a condition that affected children. I thought that people grew out of it as they learned emotional regulation, were medicated, or simply developed a tolerance to their symptoms.

What I didn't know was that ADHD is lifelong, and many of us have been living with it without ever realizing something was going on. For adult men, an ADHD diagnosis can be confusing. We've been told that having ADHD means not being able to concentrate, being hyperactive, and having problems controlling our impulses. What we're not told is that ADHD is a spectrum condition that affects people of all ages, and the symptoms of living with ADHD can vary.

For men, ADHD can present as bouts of emotional dysregulation, self-criticism, avoidant behavior, perfectionism, and depression. Our confidence takes a knock as we take on new projects only to never fully complete them. We then berate ourselves, or worse, we hurt the people we love the most.

In fact, the majority of men with ADHD did grow up with the common symptoms associated with the condition, but society deems these behaviors acceptable. Messy or disorganized bedrooms, the inability to sit still and complete tasks, or even keeping a closet tidy are all seen as typical "boy things."

Growing up like this inadvertently reinforces and rewards the behaviors associated with ADHD and ultimately compounds our disappointment in ourselves. We live for the magical moment when we will grow out of the behaviors that get us into trouble, and it's a moment that doesn't come if we never receive a diagnosis and treatment plan.

Introduction

This justifies the progression of our symptoms and behaviors until we grow up and build different relationships in which our actions, words, and mannerisms cause conflict. We begin to compensate for our difficulties and become defensive of our actions, blaming other people for nagging.

We stigmatize ourselves and become emotionally reactive, all the while intuitively knowing that something is amiss and that there has to be more to life than the whirling thoughts preoccupying our minds.

A diagnosis of ADHD can be both a source of relief and an excuse for our behavior. We can sometimes believe that we are destined to repeat the same cycle because we are broken. The reality is that you *can* thrive! You can take back your life, and you can start today.

I wrote *Mind Mapping for Men with Adult ADHD* as part of my own journey after being diagnosed with ADHD. I, too, had to learn how to stop overthinking, take accountability for my behaviors, and master my ADHD as a superpower I could use to better my career, friendships, and relationships.

When reading this book, you can expect to learn how to:

• Gain a deeper understanding of ADHD and how having it uniquely affects you as a man.

• Identify your thought spirals and how to uncover what is fueling your thoughts.

• Mind map for communication clarity and a deeper understanding of your thoughts.

• Plan and successfully take action so that you can achieve your goals.

• Improve your emotional quotient for a better relationship with yourself and others.

Finally, before you continue reading the chapters of this book, I'd like you to know that you're not alone. Men are three times more likely to be diagnosed with ADHD, although not many will seek treatment due to the stigma surrounding it. Approximately 13% of men around the globe will be on the ADHD spectrum, and only 5.4% of men will access formal treatment for their diagnosis.

Having ADHD is nothing to be ashamed of, and it doesn't have to be something that debilitates you for the remainder of your life. You have the power to positively transform your life, calm your anxious thoughts, and improve your concentration and productivity.

Part One
The ADHD Brain and Overthinking

Chapter 1

Understanding ADHD

What I need is a task. Something to concentrate on, something that will distract me from all the whirling thoughts crowding my head.

Sylvia Mercedes

Modern medicine may have become far better at diagnosing conditions, disorders, and illnesses, but most of the time, it fails to identify how these syndromes affect men and women differently.

After receiving a diagnosis, we can sometimes feel lost. A prescription in our hand and advice to see a therapist are the only guidance we are given. For some of us, instead of relief, our diagnosis can lead our thoughts to spiral and compound themselves as we ruminate about all the things we think are *wrong* with us.

For others, an ADHD diagnosis comes as a get-out-of-jail-free card for their behaviors and emotional regulation issues. These behaviors can worsen as the newly-diagnosed person feels their actions have a justifiable cause and should be free of criticism. Don't get me wrong; you have no control over your ADHD diagnosis, nor do you have control over having ADHD. However, it does not define you, and you are not a helpless victim trapped in your life and your thoughts.

As you read through this chapter, I'd like you to understand that I am not stereotyping or downplaying the struggles men with ADHD face. ADHD is complex; it falls on a spectrum, which means some of the things you read may apply to you, and others may not.

Unfortunately, ADHD is stigmatized, especially in adults and men. Society places pressure on us to have everything together and be providers for our loved ones. Certain emotions are not welcomed, so often, when we receive a diagnosis, it can become deeply rooted in shame. Defensive behaviors, emotional dysregulation, and angry outbursts can become the center of our existence, which only serves to fuel our deep feelings of inner discomfort.

ADHD in the Neurodiversity Umbrella

Neurodiversity is a word that has gained traction on social media lately, but the concept of being neurodivergent is still not properly understood. We tend to think that being neurodivergent is directly related to autism, which, in itself, is a spectrum disorder.

In reality, neurodiversity is an umbrella term used to define the common neurological characteristics of people with ADHD, autism spectrum disorder, dyslexia, dyspraxia, and dyscalculia.

The point of placing certain disorders under an umbrella term is to help remove stigma and discrimination against people who have them. However, the issue is that when we begin to define people by their condition, we're also defining them by their limitations and deficits.

Having said that, the term neurodiversity does help us to move away from labeling ADHD as a condition associated with weaknesses. It places emphasis on a person's strengths, regardless of whether or not they present with a disorder.

When it comes down to it, everyone has strengths plus weaknesses that limit them, but those who are neurodivergent tend to focus on their limitations because of what they were told when they were younger.

To embrace your ADHD and being neurodivergent, you actively need to work toward shifting your mindset. Move away from the terms "special needs" or "disorder" and toward what you can achieve with the right tools.

Regardless of whether or not you have chosen to be medicated, it's important to move away from operating out of a labeled box filled with guilt and shame.

Without first shifting your mindset and deciding that you're going to tackle ADHD head-on in a strength-based approach, you will never fully understand how focusing on your weaknesses prevents you from using your neurodivergent powers.

Neurodiversity and ADHD in Adults

Being an adult can sometimes feel like a circus juggling act, and the average adult either needs or feels obliged to keep many responsibilities going in order to be functional and successful in their lives.

From parenting to socializing, looking after our mental and physical health, and thriving in our careers, being an adult can be overwhelming, even at the best of times. For those of us with ADHD, this overwhelm can be magnified when we find ourselves constantly late, forgetful, living in disorganized chaos, or generally feeling that everything we have to get done is simply too much.

Avoidance becomes a way of life, and our frustrations manifest through dysregulated emotions, angry outbursts, and waves of anxiety and depression. Science and medicine are not convinced about the exact causes of ADHD. However, the general consensus is that it's a combination of factors, including the environment, the way our brains are hardwired, and a genetic component.

For those of us diagnosed with ADHD at a young age, some of the symptoms we experienced when we were younger will still be prevalent. We may also not be consciously aware of them, as learned behaviors and dysregulation can cause us to become blissfully unaware of our symptoms.

For others, ADHD that is carried into adulthood from childhood can continue to be debilitating. If ADHD was never diagnosed in childhood, our symptoms could feel like a curse that sets us apart from everyone else.

When ADHD is not recognized in childhood, our behaviors are often associated with negative connotations, with adults calling us unruly, defiant, lazy, or just plain bad. This reaffirms in our minds that there is something very wrong with us, and we enter into a deep state of guilt, shame, or even denial.

As a result of denial and the internal stigmas we attach to our ADHD symptoms, we can begin to run into a lot of trouble as adults, and as our responsibilities increase, we drop more and more of the juggling balls. However, it's not that we don't *know* that we need to be organized, focused, regulated, and calm; it's just that the *how* escapes us, further compounding all the negative things we think about ourselves.

The good news is that there is only one difference between adults with ADHD who are thriving and those who are not. They have learned to turn their weaknesses into strengths by accessing the right support, education, and tools.

I want you to know that it's never too late to use your ADHD to your advantage. You can learn how to succeed in life, achieve your goals, and become productive on your own terms.

Your journey to success starts with understanding your symptoms and how they may differ from what you experienced in childhood. Knowing you're not alone and gaining a deeper insight into how ADHD uniquely affects adults will help you better manage your symptoms and begin equipping you with the tools you need.

Types of ADHD

In the past, medicine and psychology recognized three types of ADHD.

These types are:

1. **Combined ADHD**: Characterized by impulsivity and hyperactivity as well as the inability to concentrate. This is the most common form of ADHD.

2. **Impulsive, hyperactive ADHD**: Characterized by impulsive and hyperactive behaviors only, without the inability to concentrate. This is the least common form of ADHD.

3. **Inattentive, distractible ADHD**: Characterized by the inability to pay attention or a high level of distractibility. This form of ADHD is more common in females.

While these three types of ADHD are the most commonly diagnosed and treated, pioneers in behavior and brain disorders have further identified other types of ADHD that can be targeted to help manage the symptoms of ADHD better.

American psychiatrist and brain disorder specialist Dr. Daniel Amen has dedicated his life's work to helping children when diagnosed with ADHD, supporting them to remove the obstacles, and giving them the tools to be successful.

One study conducted by Dr. Amen showed that each of the three types of ADHD could be further broken down into subtypes, each with its own symptoms that required special tools and treatments (Amen, 2001).

It's essential to note that Dr. Amen does not base his research purely on verbal assessments, nor does he rely solely on diagnostic tools. Instead, he uses cutting-edge brain imaging to help identify which areas of the brain are not functioning within a set of normal parameters. By identifying these areas, Dr. Amen can suggest targeted exercises and tools to help the brain work the way it should.

In addition, he discovered that ADHD may affect not only two but three of the brain's neurotransmitters. These neurotransmitters are dopamine, γ-Aminobutyric acid (GABA), and serotonin. Through imaging of the brain, he was also able to find discrepancies in various areas of the brain, not just the prefrontal cortex. In fact, these brain images showed that most of the brain was affected, including the deep structures that help create dopamine.

While Dr. Amen's theories are somewhat controversial and not recognized by medicine just yet, it's important that they are discussed so that you can use the information if you want to (Champ et al., 2021).

Following are the ADHD subtypes that Dr. Amen identified:

- **Classic ADHD** is characterized by distractibility, hyperactivity, inattentiveness, impulsivity, and disorganization.

Imaging and tests show that this type of ADHD is caused by a dopamine deficiency and not enough blood flow to the cerebellum, basal ganglia, and prefrontal cortex.

- **Inattentive ADHD** is characterized by a shortened attention span, procrastination, perfectionism, daydreaming, introversion, distractibility, and introversion.

Imaging and testing show that Inattentive ADHD is a symptom of dopamine deficiency as well as having a prefrontal cortex that is not as active as it should be.

- **Overfocused ADHD** presents with the symptoms of classic ADHD but comes with an inability to shift attention or move from task to task easily. People with overfocused ADHD can sometimes become stuck in their thought patterns and behaviors.

Imaging and testing show that this type of ADHD is a result of dopamine and serotonin deficiencies as well as an overactive cingulate gyrus in the brain.

- **Temporal Lobe ADHD** displays all of the symptoms of classic ADHD but also affects memory retention and learning. This ADHD subtype is marked by emotional outbursts, behavioral issues, and risk-taking.

Imaging shows decreased prefrontal cortex activity in those with Temporal Lobe ADHD and some abnormalities in the temporal lobe of the brain.

- **Limbic ADHD** has all of the symptoms of classic ADHD plus a chronic low mood that cannot be characterized as depression. People with Limbic ADHD may also suffer from low energy levels, low self-esteem, and have a "victim mentality."

Imaging shows increased activity in the limbic center of the brain, which affects mood, as well as a decrease in activity in the prefrontal cortex.

• **Ring of Fire ADHD** is characterized by a marked sensitivity to noise, light, and touch. People with this subtype of ADHD may lash out, behave unpredictably, or be anxious and fearful.

Imaging shows a ring of too much activity around the brain's centers, plus increased activity in the cerebral cortex and other areas at times.

• **Anxious ADHD** presents with all of the symptoms of classic ADHD but includes anxious, stressed-out behavior and the physical symptoms of stress.

Imaging shows that those with Anxious ADHD have an overactive basal ganglia, which can be confusing as other types of ADHD present with low activity in this region of the brain.

Understanding the different types of ADHD and exploring possible subtypes is important because certain medications can actually aggravate the symptoms of specific subtypes. For example, stimulant medications may increase the symptoms associated with Ring of Fire ADHD or Temporal Lobe ADHD.

How Prevalent Is ADHD in Adults

The National Institute of Mental Health study conducted in 2014 showed an overall prevalence of ADHD in adults of around 4.4%.

This percentage was taken as the median between men at 5.4% and women at 3.2%. In adults in the United States (USA), 8.1% of adults between the ages of 18 and 44 had been diagnosed with ADHD (National Institute of Mental Health, 2014).

New studies, however, show a worldwide statistic of 2.8% and only a 0.96% diagnosis in the USA, which is a big difference between the previous 4.4% and 8.1% statistics reported (Song et al., 2021).

There is some debate as to whether or not these statistics are correct, though. Those who agree with them say modern early intervention in children has significantly lowered the number of ADHD cases.

Some schools of thought are more skeptical, saying fewer people are seeking an ADHD diagnosis due to the stigma surrounding it and the bias against people with ADHD.

Diagnosis and Symptoms of ADHD in Adults Versus Kids

Adults with children who have ADHD, as well as adults who suspect they themselves have ADHD, may begin their journey to a formal diagnosis through their general practitioner (GP). While a GP cannot actually give a diagnosis, they can refer you to a specialist for assessment and further investigation into the symptoms you're experiencing. A referral usually occurs after the GP has asked some questions.

These questions will cover:

• What symptoms you are currently experiencing.

• How long you have been experiencing your symptoms.

• The frequency of your symptoms and if they become worse or better while doing certain tasks.

• How your symptoms affect your day-to-day life.

• Whether or not you're experiencing more stress than usual.

• If you have been experiencing other symptoms that could be related to a health condition.

• Your family history of mental and physical health.

From the referral stage, ADHD is handled differently, dependent on age. For children, watchful waiting is the first course of action before a referral is suggested. It is only after waiting that children will be referred to a specialist, and even then, group-based therapy and parent education classes are the preferred current frontline treatments for children with ADHD.

The reason for this is that doctors and psychologists are moving away from labeling to prevent limiting stigmas. Instead, they are opting to educate parents and children on how to overcome their weaknesses and work to their strengths. Whereas in the past, medicating children was the first line of defense against ADHD symptoms, now only the most severe and debilitating cases will be medicated.

Prescription medications need to be taken alongside therapy and education classes to give a child the best chance at managing their ADHD effectively and forming great habits to support success in adulthood.

For adults, however, the referral occurs earlier, and there is no true watchful waiting period. Your healthcare professional will use specific criteria to assess whether or not a referral is needed.

These criteria will include:

• Whether or not you had a previous ADHD diagnosis in childhood or slightly later.

• Whether or not you have been diagnosed with another mental health condition in the past.

• Whether or not your symptoms are affecting your day-to-day life. For example, are you underachieving in your job, or are your relationships suffering as a result of your symptoms?

In the past, the Diagnostic and Statistical Manual of Mental Disorders (DSM-5) was the gold standard for diagnosing mental health issues like ADHD. The DSM-5 is the standard diagnostic and classification manual used by healthcare professionals when identifying the symptoms and key traits of mental health disorders.

Lately, though, the medical and psychological fraternities have moved away from using DSM-5. The issue is that it perpetuates the notion that mental health disorders come with a genetic component when, in reality, 97% of these disorders have no known gene variants. Added to this, the DSM-5 insists that chemical imbalances are the cause of mental health disorders as a way to push pharmaceutical use (Ghaemi, 2018).

While I am not disputing that pharmaceuticals need to be used in some circumstances, there is no conclusive proof that medicine works for most mental health and behavioral disorders. The use of medications as a cure for mental health is 100% hypothetical, and pharmaceuticals are thought to mask symptoms rather than cure them.

Other issues with the DSM-5 include:

- a lack of scientific basis

- a disregard for other therapeutic methods that are based on science

- cultural bias

- a drive for pharmaceuticals as a "cure" for mental health

- the pathologizing of human experiences

- a label assigned to a person for life, limiting their experiences

As such, if you're seeing a physician for an ADHD diagnosis and have already received a previous one, you can expect a different experience.

The assessment phase of a diagnosis also varies from child to adult. A child may be referred to any one of the following specialists:

- a specialist child psychiatrist

- a pediatrician

- a child's ADHD healthcare professional

Adults will almost always be assessed by a psychiatrist and an ADHD healthcare professional. These ADHD healthcare professionals are usually general practitioners who have undergone additional training to understand the specific health needs of people with ADHD.

In most parts of the world, you can expect the following during your assessment:

- A physical exam to ascertain your general health and assert your primary healthcare physician's report on your health.

- A series of interviews with a psychiatrist, which may include different questions, exercises, and observations.

- A psychiatrist may also request to interview people who spend a lot of time with you, like your partner, friends, and family.

Once you have been thoroughly assessed, you will receive a diagnosis and a recommended treatment plan for your ADHD. Obtaining an ADHD diagnosis for a child is more difficult than for adults, as children must display more than six symptoms of attention deficit, hyperactivity, and impulsiveness.

Added to this, children must have symptoms for more than six months, have developed them prior to 12 years old, be symptomatic in different environments, and have a diminished quality of life due to their symptoms. Because of this, many children with ADHD are labeled as unruly when, in fact, they just don't fit all of the criteria listed.

Adults have fewer diagnostic criteria and usually have to show only five symptoms of attention deficit, hyperactivity, and impulsiveness. In addition, adults often have ADHD symptoms their whole lives, so they don't require a six-month waiting period.

Finally, it is a lot easier for adults to communicate that their symptoms are affecting their quality of life, which means symptoms only need to have a moderate effect on different areas of life.

These areas could include:

- underachieving in career or education

- reckless behavior with no explanation

- difficulties making or maintaining friendships

- difficulties regulating emotions

- relationship and familial difficulties

Current standards dictate that ADHD cannot develop in adulthood, and if your symptoms have only occurred later in life, there's likely another cause for what you're experiencing.

Childhood Symptoms

An inability to concentrate, hyperactive behaviors, and impulsivity are the hallmark symptoms of ADHD in both adults and children. It's important to remember that ADHD is a spectrum condition, which means you may have some symptoms working together to create an imbalance in your life, or you may be experiencing all of them.

In other words, you may find it difficult to concentrate but not be impulsive, particularly hyperactive, or you may be incredibly hyperactive and impulsive but can hyper-focus and concentrate pretty well.

Childhood ADHD usually presents with one or more of the following symptoms, which range from mild to severe:

• Uncontrollable fidgeting, wiggling, or foot tapping.

• An inability to stay seated even for short periods of time.

• An inability to wait—blurting out answers, pushing in lines, or shoving people aside.

• Outward displays of insatiable energy and a preference for running and climbing.

• An inability to remain quiet, even for short periods.

• A preference for gross motor skill activities over fine motor skill activities.

• Fine motor skills deficits.

• Excessive talking or talking for no reason.

• An inability to respect personal space.

Biologically, female children are more likely not to be diagnosed with ADHD, as symptoms and behaviors are more subtle but no less debilitating than those of their male counterparts.

Adulthood Symptoms

For most adults, hyperactivity is not an outward symptom of ADHD. This doesn't mean adults don't experience hyperactivity that they repress; it's just that it usually drives different behaviors than in kids, like emotional outbursts. For some adults with ADHD, poor coping mechanisms have been learned, and symptoms can present as other mental health issues, including perfectionism, defiance, or anger management issues.

In adults, symptoms of ADHD almost always co-occur, which means adults will have three or, most likely, all of the symptoms listed below:

• Feelings of restlessness or pent-up energy.

• Attention is focused on being calm and still, meaning they are unaware of other things happening.

• Impatience can result in emotional outbursts.

• Emotional dysregulation.

• An inability to allow others to finish their sentences or be quick to argue.

• Displays reckless behaviors without consideration for others at the moment but feels remorse afterward.

• Decreased tolerance for stress and frustration.

• Excessive talking.

• Can make inappropriate comments.

• An inability to complete tasks, sometimes seen as procrastination.

• Messy, untidy, and forgetful.

• Sometimes seems to be "operating" automatically.

• Anxiety and depression.

Brain fog, spacing out, being late, and feeling like mistakes are fatal can all compound anxiety and depression in adults with ADHD.

Essentially, adult ADHD affects how well we can pay attention, whereas childhood ADHD affects how well we can train ourselves to pay attention. In childhood, ADHD presents ways to release pent-up energy, which is why kids with ADHD don't learn to concentrate and focus on the task at hand.

The Causes and Risk Factors of ADHD

To date, there has been no official conclusion as to the cause of ADHD. While some studies show there may be a genetic component, others can disprove this. The brain is a wonderfully complex organ, and there is still so much to learn about how it functions or what causes it to behave differently in people.

While parenting and the home environment definitely play some role in the behaviors a person learns, not all ADHD can be attributed to environmental factors. The nature versus nurture debate simply doesn't apply when it comes to neurodivergent conditions. A lot of the time, children can come from homes with no abuse or neglect, and a child may be diagnosed with ADHD or the like.

The fact that nature versus nurture doesn't apply to ADHD further compounds the question, "What causes ADHD?" Science is taking on this question by looking at the risks associated with the development of ADHD in children rather than trying to pin down any one underlying cause.

Brain Function or Anatomy that Is Altered or Different

Studies have been done to determine whether the way an ADHD brain functions is different from the way an average brain looks and operates. One such study focused on the brain activity of children and adults with ADHD. These studies revealed that people with ADHD have a frontal lobe that is different from people who do not have ADHD. The frontal lobe is responsible for our decision-making processes, voluntary movements, expressive language, and executive-level functioning. This study also showed differences in the arrangement of neurotransmitters, including noradrenaline and dopamine transmitters, the chemical messengers in the brain (Mayo Clinic, 2019).

Hereditary or Genetic Component

Research has both proven and disproven a genetic component in ADHD. However, new studies are investigating whether or not the condition may be caused by a combination of parental genetics or gene mutations (Balogh et al., n.d.).

Biological Gender

Statistics suggest that people who are born biological males are more likely to develop ADHD. It is theorized that hormonal and genetic factors may pose a risk when it comes to the development of ADHD.

Having said that, since boys are more likely to be impulsive and hyperactive, it's thought that girls are often not diagnosed. Treatment is never sought because girls are labeled as 'scatterbrained' or 'eccentric' as their symptoms present differently. It seems that the inability to concentrate and forgetfulness are the two symptoms both genders have in common, even in adulthood.

Fetal Exposure to Alcohol, Drugs, and Tobacco Smoke

Exposure to substances like alcohol, drugs, and tobacco smoke may be a risk factor for the development of ADHD in childhood. While studies do suggest a link between maternal health and well-being during pregnancy, nothing solid has been established, and no pathology has been discovered.

Again, most theories surrounding fetal exposure are hypothesized; however, it would appear that abuse of substances affects the nerve messengers within a fetus's brain. Added to this, exposure to environmental toxins may also be a contributing factor to neurotransmitter function and arrangement in people who do not have ADHD.

Exposure to Environmental Toxins in Childhood

In a world that seems to be filled with artificial flavors, preservatives, and sterile environments that coincide with the rise of ADHD in children, studies are being done into the effect of environmental toxins as a risk factor for ADHD. Lead exposure from paint and pipes has been shown to change behaviors in children, sometimes causing shorter attention spans and even violent outbursts (Donzelli et al., 2019).

Traumatic Brain Injury (TBI)

TBIs are injuries to the brain that are so severe that they alter the function of the brain. A TBI is caused by external forces like falls and accidents. Some studies show a small correlation between TBIs and the onset of ADHD in childhood, although none of these studies are definitive (Asarnow et al., 2021).

Foods Including Additives, Preservatives, Sugar, and Food Intolerances

While some foods that contain additives and preservatives have been shown to worsen the symptoms of ADHD, there is also some evidence that these chemicals could increase the risk of ADHD in children.

Refined sugars have also been linked with behavioral issues in children. Although studies have shown that there is no real association between sugar intake and the development of ADHD, sugar may escalate the symptoms of it.

In addition, children who suffer from food intolerances to common, healthy foods like milk, nuts, and wheat may be at an increased risk of developing ADHD due to the poor absorption of nutrition in the gut (Ryu et al., 2022).

Exposure to Television from a Young Age

There is some evidence that children who are exposed to long periods in front of the television may have an increased risk of developing ADHD. While studies on screen time are inconclusive, there is a correlation between screen time and attention deficits or the inability to sit still when the brain is not being actively stimulated (Stevens, 2006).

Intrauterine Growth Restriction (IUGR) and Premature Birth

Some studies show that babies born prior to 37 weeks of gestation, those born with low birth weight, or those diagnosed with IUGR are more likely to develop ADHD later in childhood. In addition, micro preemies (babies born extremely early and small) who suffer from brain bleeding at birth or after birth may have an increased risk of ADHD (Montagna et al., 2020).

As you can see, ADHD *could* be caused by a number of different things, but no conclusive or definitive proof has been discovered as to one specific risk or cause.

Common Misconceptions About Adult ADHD

Despite the amount of research and brain imaging findings that show ADHD results from neurological deficits or irregularities in the brain, ADHD is still massively stigmatized. When any condition is stigmatized, it comes with myths. These myths need to be dispelled to lift the guilt, shame, and sometimes blame that people carry around with them once they have been diagnosed.

Myth 1: ADHD Is Not a Disorder

This simply isn't true. Psychological, medical, and educational organizations all agree that ADHD is a legitimate medical condition. Where some confusion may come in is that certain institutions classify ADHD as a mental disorder, whereas others see it as a behavioral disorder. Regardless, ADHD is a medical condition that requires treatment to improve a person's quality of life.

Myth 2: ADHD Is Caused by Parenting

While upbringing and environmental factors do seem to play a small role in kids with ADHD, there is no conclusive proof that behavioral disorders are a result of a lack of discipline or parenting style. Even kids with overly strict parents may be diagnosed with ADHD, and may be more highly stigmatized by society because they are punished by their parent for behaviors they don't know how to manage.

Myth 3: ADHD Is a Male Condition

While it is true that more boys are diagnosed with ADHD than girls, gender does not play a part in how many people have ADHD. This myth persists because boys more often display disruptive, outward symptoms such as hyperactivity and disruptive behaviors that disrupt their classmates. In adults, men are more prone to have symptoms of risk-taking behavior and angry outbursts.

All of these symptoms mean males are more inclined to try to find a reason for their disruptive behaviors. On the other hand, females, who have more internally disruptive behaviors, are more likely to be diagnosed with a mood or personality disorder.

Myth 4: People with ADHD Cannot Be Successful

Again, this is absolutely not true. If history has taught us anything, it's that ADHD, when managed and channeled properly, doesn't need to be a hindrance, and anyone can be successful. In fact, some of the most influential and successful people of all time, including Mozart, Salvador Dali, Richard Branson, and George Bernard Shaw, all had or have ADHD.

Myth 5: Adult ADHD Doesn't Exist

There is a pretty common myth that children outgrow ADHD, and as such, adult ADHD doesn't exist. The reality is that more than 70% of children with ADHD will continue to experience symptoms throughout their teen years, and about 50% will have ADHD in adulthood (Wilens & Spencer, 2010).

Now that you have a better understanding of ADHD and have dispelled some of the myths surrounding the condition, we can move on to how ADHD affects men specifically and the symptoms that drive our behaviors.

Chapter 2

Adult ADHD in Men

Anxiety does not empty tomorrow of its sorrows, but only empties today of its strength.

Charles Spurgeon

Previous research suggested that ADHD does not affect males and females differently, and as such, mainstream treatments of ADHD were generic and did not focus on any specific set of symptoms.

Modern research, however, indicates that ADHD *does* affect biological males and females differently and that the type and severity of symptoms can differ between genders.

Psychiatry focuses on symptoms as a whole, which is probably why previous research suggested that ADHD presents the same way in males and females. In contrast, psychology focuses on shared human experiences rather than a set of symptoms.

Consequently, psychologists are at the forefront of changing attitudes regarding ADHD and how it affects males and females differently. For science to truly understand ADHD and create a system that is genuinely effective in managing its symptoms, there needs to be an acknowledgment that ADHD affects men and women in different ways.

How ADHD Differs in Men and Women

Before we explore how ADHD symptoms differ in men and women, we must take a look at how the frequency of a diagnosis can affect overall statistics and the reporting of symptoms.

Because boys are more likely to be diagnosed due to the disruptive symptoms they display, it can appear that males have an increased disposition toward developing ADHD. However, the reality is that the female symptoms are more introspective and less disruptive, meaning women are more likely to be misdiagnosed or completely overlooked when it comes to ADHD. This also means that females are less likely to receive medication or referrals to therapy, which would help them manage their symptoms.

Cultural attitudes toward boys and girls also influence how many children will be diagnosed with ADHD, as "boys will be boys" and "girls are eccentric and scatterbrained" biases continue to permeate our society.

In women, ADHD is also seemingly misdiagnosed more often than in men. This misdiagnosis could be because of female hormones, which play a role in fluctuating mood and altering brain chemistry throughout the course of the female reproductive cycle. It is thought that certain ADHD symptoms can be compounded by these hormones.

Regardless of a person's gender, an adult diagnosis of ADHD is far more complex than one in childhood. While there are fewer criteria to meet, healthcare professionals will have more comorbidities to consider before a diagnosis is given.

ADHD in Men

Men may present with some of the inattentive symptoms that women do, but generally speaking, men are more likely to have the outward disruptive symptoms of ADHD.

For males, the unique symptoms of ADHD are:

• outward hyperactive behavior

• disruptive displays of behavior

• forgetfulness and losing items

• interrupting

• outward displays of aggression

- participating in high-risk behaviors, including substance abuse and risky sexual behavior

- insensitivity toward others' emotions

While these symptoms are usually present in men, this doesn't mean that women don't sometimes have one or more of them. Having said that, men are far more likely to engage in these behaviors than women, and most men will have feelings of guilt and shame as a result of what they have done.

More common symptoms that can be experienced by both men and women include:

- difficulty sitting still or concentrating for long periods

- procrastination

- an inability to follow through with committed tasks

- not being able to manage time properly

- poor emotional regulation

- difficulty or inability to handle criticism or rejection

- an inability to identify risks or consequences

- difficulty putting their thoughts into words or actions

- frustration

- feelings of restlessness or wanting to fidget at all times

- an inability to follow a conversation or interrupt to change the course of a conversation

Intensity of Symptoms

What different scientific approaches do agree on is that the intensity of symptoms between men and women differs, although they haven't quite figured out why. The magnitude of hyperactivity seems to be far greater in males than in females, and the intensity of inattentiveness is more prevalent in females.

It is believed that the manifestations of symptoms often rely heavily on the societal roles people play due to their upbringing and the social environments they grow up in. This certainly seems to be true with men when it comes to relationship issues, risk-taking behaviors, and outwardly aggressive or disruptive behaviors.

We live in a world where it is okay for men to be aggressive or take risks, but it is not okay for them to speak about their feelings or be anxious. As a result, young boys with ADHD can grow into men who don't know how to manage or even identify their symptoms properly.

How the ADHD Brain Works

The ADHD brain doesn't only work differently from neurotypical brains; magnetic resonance imaging (MRI) shows that the development, function, and structure of ADHD brains are different.

These differences are what cause ADHD symptoms and the patterns of behavior that we form as a way of coping with our symptoms. For those of us with ADHD, our brain networks, size, and neurotransmitters don't function like other people's. Some areas of our brain can either over-function or under-function when they shouldn't.

A number of these differences may correct themselves or change from childhood through adolescence and finally into adulthood, which would account for the myth that people "grow out" of ADHD.

The reality is that the brain needs to be taught to change and how to function in certain ways. While it is possible for us to develop fresh neurons and neurotransmitters, we need to learn new things for these not to replicate themselves in their old forms.

In the past, it was thought that neuroplasticity, or the ability to create fresh neural pathways, was lost after adolescence. While it is true that kids learn new things a lot easier than adults due to the maturation processes in the brain, neuroplasticity is never lost. We can learn additional behaviors and information throughout our whole lives.

This means all is not lost when it comes to adult ADHD and is also why behavioral therapies like cognitive behavioral therapy (CBT) are so effective in helping to manage ADHD. For us to understand the ADHD brain, though, we first need to take a deeper look into how the function and structure of neurodiverse brains differ from neurotypical ones.

Functional Differences

The functioning of the brain is affected by ADHD in several ways that directly impact our cognitive, behavioral, and self-motivating processes. Added to this, certain types and intensities of ADHD may affect how well we regulate our emotions, feelings, and moods.

Emotions are a physiological function; everyone has them, and they're an evolutionary response we have developed to keep us safe. Emotions are fleeting and last around 90 seconds before fading away. Once we experience an emotion, we can decide to manage and eliminate it or prolong how we feel about it for a short while. Alternatively, we can choose to dwell on and stretch out these feelings, allowing them to affect our entire day, week, month, or even life!

Feelings and moods are choices; emotions are not. Anger can turn to irritation, and irritation can turn to, "My life is so hard, and everyone is against me!"

Because ADHD may affect how we respond to our emotions, it can also more dramatically affect our feelings and mood. We feel guilt or shame for our emotional outbursts and are unable to manage our emotions in the moment. For people with ADHD, the brain network is structurally altered, meaning it takes more time to develop. It also means it takes more effort to relay messages on what we should do with our emotions, behaviors, movement, focus, etc.

Added to this, certain regions of the ADHD brain can be either hyper-active or hypoactive, so no balance or regulation is happening in response to stimuli. The issue with only medicating ADHD is that we are never afforded the opportunity to correct our behaviors while consciously overriding the functional differences in our brains. This means we never learn the right coping mechanisms, nor do we stimulate the development of new neural pathways that will help us sustain fresh, positive behaviors.

Structural Differences

The ADHD brain has several structural differences when compared with neurotypical brains. Almost all of these differences can affect how a person behaves or reacts to their environment and the people they are interacting with.

These structural differences include a brain that is slightly smaller than neurotypical ones, with slower maturation rates, and volume differences in the amygdala and hippocampus areas of the brain. It's important to know that brain structure doesn't affect intelligence in the least, only the ability to process information at what society deems to be a 'normal rate.'

Structural differences in the brain may affect how well we regulate our emotions and recall memories from our subconscious and our level of self-motivation. The frontal cortex, which is responsible for our ability to concentrate, plan, and perform other cognitive functions, is most affected by maturation differences. This could be why restlessness and fidgeting will increase, and time management will be affected when we have ADHD.

The motor cortex, which controls movement in the body, is often more mature in people with ADHD, which is why kids with ADHD usually do really well in sports if they are allowed to focus on these skills.

These structural and functional differences in the brain are what define ADHD as a behavioral and not a mental health condition. And this brings us full circle to the DSM-5, which deals with mental disorders.

In addition, these differences in the ADHD brain suggest that the condition should be treated based on behavioral and mindset changes, with medical assistance where needed. ADHD cannot be medicated away, but yes, medication may be needed to help some people function. However, you need to be willing to work on your behavior, practice self-love and acceptance as you rehearse your new skills, and take action every day. This will help your brain rewire itself so that you can manage your symptoms more effectively.

Common Challenges Men With ADHD Face

Men with ADHD face specific challenges that are mainly unique to them. While I don't want to stereotype any one gender, it's important to know which challenges are most specific to men with ADHD, so you know what behaviors you should be working on.

If you tied your shoelaces wrong your whole life and the laces came undone, frustrated you, and caused you to fall and hurt yourself or others, wouldn't you want to know that you were tying them wrong?

Psychologists who work with men with ADHD have identified certain patterns of behavior that impact their quality of life and that of the people they are friends or in relationships with. These commonalities are pretty vast, but the most typical of them are listed below.

Career and Work

For many men, their identity is wrapped up in their profession and ability to provide the lifestyle they think they deserve. While there is nothing wrong with basing some of your identity on your job, it can become an issue for men with ADHD, as behaviors that are not addressed can cause problems at work.

Many men with ADHD find that they are fired from their dream jobs, constantly on the edge of disciplinary action, or isolated from their peers, which creates an unpleasant work environment.

A lot of these outcomes are consequences of ADHD behavior that has not been addressed. Not finishing tasks, having to be micromanaged to get work done, emotional outbursts, and interrupting people in meetings or while they talk can all negatively compound over time.

Other ADHD symptoms that can affect work are:

- forgetfulness

- impulsivity

- poor timekeeping

- disorganization

Often, men with ADHD also display some form of defiance, as their ego seeks to protect them from feeling shame and guilt for their behaviors. This defiance is often the driving factor behind men with ADHD being fired. This pressure to achieve goals can lead to slacking off work, which is directly interpreted by leaders as willful misconduct or non-compliance.

Time Management

Distraction, fixation, forgetfulness, and the inability to anticipate the consequences of actions can all lead to poor time management and procrastination, ultimately resulting in productivity becoming static.

Men with ADHD are not natural planners and, as such, have issues with deadlines. As more and more tasks pile up, defiance and defensive behaviors can begin to be used as a shield against why tasks haven't been completed.

Because ADHD is a behavioral condition that affects our executive functions, we can tend to live too much in the present and not enough in the future. This means we have a hard time understanding what the rewards are for getting a task done, preferring to fill our lives with instant gratification.

This tendency can cause issues for us as our friends and partners become frustrated with us for being constantly late or not following through with our commitments. Of course, it also affects work performance, as procrastination often means failing to achieve the goals set for us.

Disorganization and Clutter

Some people with ADHD do well with clutter and disorganization, while others can get lost in the mess they have created. It can sometimes be difficult to figure out whether or not the clutter and disorganization created are causing more harm than good.

Here's a good measure of whether you are organized or not. If your controlled chaos wastes time while you look for things, slows down your ability to get tasks done, or creates an unhygienic environment, it's no longer organized. Disorganization and clutter are hallmarks of ADHD that follow most children into adulthood.

Some kids learn how to deal well with chaos and disorganization. When they become adults, this disorganization brings them comfort and actually increases their ability to get tasks done. However, others are swallowed up by their disorganization, which affects everything from their job to their relationships. A good benchmark for assessing whether clutter and disorganization are beneficial to you is to ask, "Is this costing me time?"

Risk-Taking

When we take risks, adrenaline is released into our bodies, and this hormone surge can also signal our brains to release dopamine. Because the neurons that respond to dopamine are often not fully mature in people with ADHD, more dopamine is needed for them to feel the effects of being happy or content. As such, people with ADHD may take risks so that they can increase their feelings of well-being.

Risk-taking behavior can be further compounded by not fully understanding or thinking about the consequences of their actions, which can lead to impulsive and reckless actions. To learn how to better control your impulsive behavior with the ABC Model, download your free bonus!

It's important to note that risk-taking behavior can range from minor to severe. Being late for events, interrupting conversations, or picking petty fights with your partner may all be part of your risk-taking behavior.

Severe risk-taking behaviors like driving dangerously or too fast, abusing substances, infidelity, and committing crimes are usually escalations of minor risks taken at a younger age. If you are participating in severe risk-taking behavior, this is something that needs to be addressed by a medical professional as soon as possible. There are much safer and healthier ways for people to balance dopamine production and uptake that should be discussed with a healthcare professional as a matter of urgency.

Sleep

While poor sleep is often not listed as one of the symptoms of ADHD, men specifically say that their sleep is incredibly poor as a result of the condition. The reasons for bad sleep range from having too many thoughts whirling around to rumination, restlessness, too much energy, or overstimulation. In fact, more than 80% of men with ADHD report having trouble falling asleep and staying asleep at night (Pera, 2022).

Sexual Infidelity

Many men value their performance in the bedroom and use their sexual performance as a key influencer of how high or low their self-esteem is. Having ADHD can affect sexual performance by making it harder for a man to please his partner. This leads to feelings of failure and ultimately drives the need to improve their self-esteem through other means.

When risk-taking behavior and impulsivity are brought into the equation, men with ADHD may begin to develop poor habits that destroy relationships. Online pornography, strip clubs, extramarital affairs or cheating, and engaging in unprotected sex all come with very serious consequences that men with ADHD often don't think about.

Afterward, however, these consequences can become very real, and anxiety and depression can threaten to overcome a person, leading to suicidal ideation. Studies show that men with ADHD who are not actively working on their behaviors are 50% more likely to participate in sexually risky behavior and infidelity (Sarkis, 2011).

Less Treatment

Men are taught from a young age that the behaviors surrounding ADHD are "guy things" and that what they're experiencing is normal, which could not be further from the truth. As a result, many men with ADHD will never seek treatment, nor will they speak about how the challenges they're facing are causing them emotional hurt and harm.

In addition, the stigma surrounding mental health and the misplaced perception that ADHD is a mental health disorder can mean men are more likely to suffer in silence when it comes to ADHD. Of course, this compounds many of the issues men face when dealing with ADHD. Ultimately, a man can lead himself to believe that it is just his "lot" in life: to suffer instead of thrive. ADHD is not a condition that corrects itself.

While many men have learned adequate or even great coping mechanisms for dealing with the symptoms of ADHD, there are a whole lot more who are genuinely suffering needlessly.

ADHD Men in Relationships

Men with ADHD can present with two extremes when dealing with relationship conflict. They can become very easily annoyed and animated in their irritation and anger, or they can become conflict-avoidant, which develops passive-aggressive behaviors. Both extremes can be very detrimental to personal and romantic relationships, negatively impacting the person with ADHD and those on the receiving end.

Additionally, romantic relationships can become strained due to a lack of attention to detail, messiness, and having to be constantly reminded to do small tasks. Significant others may feel like they're being neglected or that their role has shifted from a life partner to a parental role as they are constantly managing their ADHD man's behaviors and mess.

When relationship troubles begin to arise for ADHD men, they may have difficulty expressing what it is they're going through or how they feel. In turn, this can be extremely frustrating for their partners.

Up to 70% of men with ADHD suffer from emotional dysregulation that can cause angry outbursts, often directed at unsuspecting partners (Beheshti et al., 2020). Emotional dysregulation can also create a dopamine feedback loop in which ADHD men seek out conflict behavior as a way to stimulate brain activity.

For ADHD men in relationships, this can create a negative behavior pattern. A calm and peaceful relationship is replaced with a game of drama and problem creation so that they can build excitement and feel better temporarily.

Of course, this is highly detrimental to any relationship as it erodes intimacy and creates a toxic relationship environment. As a result of emotional dysregulation and the creation of problems, many men with ADHD are wrongly labeled as narcissists.

While having ADHD doesn't excuse abusive behavior, knowing why you may be creating a problem in your relationship can help you fix the very behaviors eroding your intimate connection with your partner.

ADHD Comorbidities

ADHD changes a person's life, and receiving a positive diagnosis gives them an opportunity to improve their quality of life. Whether through medication, therapy, or a combination of these two treatment options, alongside dietary changes, exercise, and a willingness to change, ADHD can be very effectively managed.

While most people with ADHD may need to fine-tune their treatment plan until they're doing well in their lives, others may find that no matter how hard they work, they're still battling with their ADHD. The reason for this is not ADHD itself but the fact that almost half of all people with ADHD have a comorbid condition (Silver, 2023). Comorbid means that more than one condition is occurring simultaneously.

Comorbid conditions that affect men with ADHD include:

- anxiety

- depression

- obsessive-compulsive disorder (OCD)

- oppositional defiant disorder (ODD)

- difficulties learning

- gross and fine motor skills difficulties

- executive function difficulties

- tic disorders

Most of the time, these disorders are the primary cause of the symptoms of ADHD, and as such, only co-occurring symptoms of both conditions will get better with treatment. Other times, secondary disorders are triggered by prolonged exposure to ADHD symptoms. For example, a person may suffer from chronic anxiety as a result of not being able to perform due to their anxiety. Alternatively, someone may develop depression because they feel guilt, shame, or fear that they will not succeed in life. A person is usually diagnosed with a comorbid condition when the symptoms of ADHD are not sufficiently resolved with treatment.

Generally speaking, there are three ADHD comorbidity categories:

1. Cortical wiring disabilities include learning, language, fine and gross motor, and executive functioning difficulties.

These comorbid conditions can be rectified with proper lifestyle changes and behavioral therapy; they do not usually require medication.

2. Emotional regulation disabilities include depression, anxiety, anger control, OCD, ODD, and bipolar disorder.

These conditions require professional medical intervention and medication to help correct chemical imbalances in the brain and body. ADHD is usually a secondary condition to these, and medications need to be properly prescribed and monitored by a psychiatrist or physician.

3. Tic disorders that include motor and oral tics, as well as Tourette's syndrome, are disabilities that are not common but can occur due to certain ADHD medications.

Throat clearing and physical tics are typical side effects of medicines like methylphenidate (Ritalin and Concerta) and mixed amphetamine salts (Adderall and Mydayis).

A healthcare professional will lower the dose of these ADHD medications or stop treatment altogether to see if tic symptoms improve. If they do not, a comorbid condition will be diagnosed.

The Strengths of ADHD and How to Use Them to Your Advantage

So much emphasis is placed on ADHD as a disorder or a weakness. The reality is that with every weakness comes strength. It is the law of nature that everything created must have balance for it to work effectively. It is our weaknesses that make us unique, and our strengths allow us to balance out the things that don't work all that well for us.

Even neurotypical people have weaknesses. The difference is that people who do not have a diagnosis for a condition or disorder don't usually focus on their deficiencies. To harness our strengths, we need to do the same: Focus on what makes us unique and tap into our ADHD superpowers to help us overcome our weaknesses. When we learn to tap into our strengths while working on our weaknesses, we can turn our ADHD into a formidable ally that drives our success.

ADHD Hyperfocus

Not everyone has the ability to hyperfocus on tasks without ever having to take a break, and even fewer people can tune out the world to immerse themselves in what they are doing.

For people with ADHD, hyperfocus usually occurs when they are doing something they find really interesting, enjoying themselves, or have set their minds to completing a task. With ADHD hyperfocus, task completion can be used to improve productivity, work more efficiently, and outperform neurotypical people. Fewer distractions also mean that the quality of what is produced in a hyperfocused state is often far better than other neurotypical people's work.

Resilience

A growth mindset, in which we believe we can achieve anything we set our mind to, requires resilience. Without resilience, we can give up too easily or spend too much time analyzing why things aren't working rather than noting why our task failed and then trying again.

People with ADHD have had to overcome many obstacles in life, facing rejection and failure more often than neurotypical people. As such, those with ADHD are far more likely to be resilient to difficulties. Setbacks and adversity are a part of life for people who are neurodivergent, and when resilience is tapped into, just about any obstacle can be overcome.

Ridding ourselves of a "victim mentality" and choosing to use our ADHD in our favor will help us tap into our resilience and ensure we can work past our setbacks efficiently. Additionally, resilience builds a strong mental character that other people look to for guidance and inspiration.

Some of the best leaders and most successful entrepreneurs, like Richard Branson and Ingvar Kamprad (the founder of Ikea), have received an ADHD diagnosis. However, these people didn't dwell on their weaknesses, instead choosing to work within their strengths and resilience.

The trick with resilience is to become deeply self-aware of our behavior to know when we're the cause of the issues around us and when something is happening to us. When we become self-aware, we can identify what needs to be worked on and take the necessary steps toward success.

Creativity

One of the hallmark strengths of ADHD is creativity and the ability to approach goal-oriented tasks from a different perspective than neurotypical people. Having ADHD and living with it throughout childhood requires finding alternative solutions to the common issues and problems life can present. This different approach means people with ADHD inherently become amazing problem-solvers and can often come up with multiple solutions to one issue.

Impactful Conversational Skills

Most boys with ADHD will be described as excessively talkative, and this trait is often carried through to adulthood. However, because men with ADHD have learned over time what is acceptable in conversation and what is not, they have fine-tuned their conversational skills. Additionally, as people with ADHD are creative and take on problems differently from others, their conversations are often interesting and engaging.

While men with ADHD may have lower emotional intelligence, they have a much higher level of social intelligence in comparison with their neurotypical counterparts. All of this means those with ADHD have the ability to become profoundly impactful masters of speech and can use this skill to make a difference in the world.

Courage

People with ADHD have to overcome a lot in their lives so they can live peacefully with self-love and acceptance. Along with building resilience, courage is a byproduct of overcoming these challenges. Over time, learning courage and the ability to ascertain the difference between good and bad risks can help men with ADHD become highly sought-after employees.

Instead of overthinking situations, people with ADHD who have learned to assess risk quickly will make a decision and work through any obstacles resulting from that choice.

Boundless Energy

Another one of the hallmark traits of men with ADHD is a lot of energy. Whether this energy is internalized or not is irrelevant, and when men can learn to use this energy constructively, they can often outperform their colleagues at work.

This energy is also why so many men with ADHD excel in sports and other recreational activities. When creating a balance between focus and ways to burn off this energy in a constructive way, men with ADHD can truly use their superpowers to their advantage. The trick with ADHD is to stop focusing on the weaknesses the condition presents and start looking at all of the amazing strengths it has to offer.

For many people, ADHD has been the greatest gift they have received because they have learned to use their neurodiverse brains to their advantage. Like other conditions, ADHD is only disabling if you allow it to be. It's important to remember that ADHD does not define you; *you* define how you will use it to your advantage.

How to Overcome the Stigma and Shame of ADHD

I'm sure people have told you that there is absolutely nothing wrong with receiving an ADHD diagnosis. Yet these words often don't come with comfort as societal stigmas continue circulating, leading to deep feelings of fear, guilt, and shame.

We can begin to think that we are flawed and weak rather than seeing all we have overcome to get to this point in our lives. Feeling shame about being diagnosed with ADHD is counterproductive as it highlights perceived weaknesses instead of strengths.

Receiving your ADHD diagnosis is a blessing. It lets you know that your unique brain can be used to your advantage and helps you specifically identify weaknesses that you can work on. However, if you are battling with your diagnosis, here are some ways you can overcome the stigma and shame that accompany ADHD.

Find a Mentor or Read About Other ADHD Men's Successes

Believe it or not, thousands of people around the world have received an ADHD diagnosis, and many of these people are incredibly successful. Instead of focusing on all the negative things people are saying, it's important that you also seek out success stories. That way, you can not only find the commonalities in any symptoms you may be experiencing but also see how other people used these symptoms to their advantage.

Seeking out someone who can mentor you is also a great way to help you identify where you may be battling and uncover areas of strength. A mentor with ADHD will also allow you to relate better to their struggles and form a bond with someone equally unique.

Surrounding yourself with information and educating yourself on other people's successes will also help you understand that ADHD doesn't mean you're broken. You're just different, and uniqueness is a sought-after trait.

When you do have moments of feeling low, remind yourself that some of the greatest and most creative minds in history used their ADHD to entertain, educate, and invent, making others' lives better and happier.

Set Aside the Victim Mentality

I know it's a harsh realization, but everyone has their own struggles, some smaller than yours and others much larger. Going through struggles is part of life, and without setting aside your victim mentality, you'll never be able to see your strengths or utilize them to your advantage. With tenacity, knowledge, and an embrace of your diagnosis, you could potentially be unstoppable.

When You Feel Weak, Highlight Your Strengths

No one denies that ADHD comes with frustrations and weaknesses, but it also comes with many strengths you can take advantage of. It's important to understand that when it is channeled properly, ADHD can be your greatest strength, and it can actually accelerate your journey to achieving your goals. Of course, there will be days when you feel frustrated and down because you're battling against yourself, but in these moments, it's a good idea to remind yourself of all your other strengths.

Be Accountable

Once you have received your diagnosis, you're presented with a choice: To become responsible for your own future and health and be accountable for your actions, or to live the rest of your life using your ADHD as an excuse for your behaviors.

For anyone to overcome stigma and take control of their lives, they first need to acknowledge that a problem exists and then look for solutions to this problem.

Is your journey to success going to be perfect?

No!

Are you going to stumble and make mistakes along the way, slipping into old habits from time to time?

Yes!

But this doesn't mean you're not responsible for being accountable when it comes to your own journey in life. Becoming accountable for your actions and life will mean you spend less time on things that are not productive for your future and more time on improving your life. You will begin to understand the impact your actions have on others. You will also start to value everything you have overcome while celebrating all the milestones you have achieved so far.

Once you become accountable, your confidence will begin to soar as you realize that stigmas mean nothing if you pay no attention to them. Finally, overcoming the stigma of ADHD requires you to step outside of a negative mindset and embrace all the positive things the world has to offer. You need to be able to work on your own thoughts before you can change other people's outlooks on what ADHD is and how it affects those who have it.

Working on your thoughts and ensuring that you are developing effective coping mechanisms, building your self-esteem, and practicing emotional intelligence will change your actions, and actions always speak louder than words. Over time, you will begin to prove to yourself that your ADHD is less of a disability and more of a superpower that you have been blessed with.

Your ADHD is absolutely not a curse, nor is it a disease that you need to feel any guilt or shame for. You have the same, if not more, opportunities to succeed as so many other people. It all begins with how you choose to manage your thoughts.

Chapter 3

Your Thought Spiral

> You don't have to control your thoughts; you just have to stop letting them control you.
>
> Dan Millman

Overthinking isn't necessarily a bad thing. Everyone has moments where they may overthink a situation before taking action, but it can become an issue and potentially create a much larger problem for you.

Being stuck in our thoughts is a symptom of ADHD, drawing our time and attention into scenarios that may or may not be true. Overthinking traps us in a never-ending spiral, repeating the same thought and applying it to different situations without any end goal or aim.

Under normal circumstances, overthinking can be halted by consciously choosing another topic and switching to it so that you can move on. In the ADHD brain, though, changing to a new topic can have you applying the old topic to the new one, forcing you to process the same thought over and over again in every situation.

Being stuck in a thought spiral is detrimental to our mental health, not only because it takes up our time, but also because it can, over time, begin to be the root cause of depression and frustration.

Unfortunately, ruminating thoughts are also a metaphorical magnet in our brain, pulling in one bad memory after the next and driving us to relive everything negative that has happened in our lives.

Because the ADHD brain works differently from the neurotypical brain and certain areas of the brain can be overly active, overthinking can be a symptom of the condition. When overthinking persists and a person allows rumination to overtake their life, comorbid conditions like OCD can occur.

The Side Effects of Overthinking and ADHD

Overthinking can come with a lot of unpleasant side effects; some, like depression and losing time, have already been discussed. Almost all of the side effects of overthinking are not great, and the five most common of these are listed below.

1. **We begin to isolate ourselves from people**: Rumination can make us believe that people don't like us or that our ADHD is a burden to others. As a result, we begin to remove ourselves from society. Over-discussing every situation and conversation we have is exhausting, to say the least, so instead of putting ourselves through that, we start to feel that it would be better if we were alone.

Additionally, when we ruminate, we may perceive other people's actions or words as hurtful without considering their intent or empathizing with what they are going through. Instead, we lash out and become hurtful, forcing others to stay away from us.

2. **We begin to lose confidence**: A lot of the time, when we ruminate, our thoughts aren't about what others have done but about what *we* have done. We start to focus on our mistakes, leading us to lose confidence in our abilities. Replaying our mistakes repeatedly, even if we only made this mistake once, can make us feel like we've made an endless number of mistakes when, in reality, we're just as imperfect as the next person.

3. **Our body begins to react physically**: When stress levels go up, our mental and physical health takes a beating. Subjecting our minds to stressful thoughts and reliving these stressful moments creates a situation in which our body remains in a stress response. Being stuck in this stress response increases blood pressure and heart rate and lowers our immune system.

4. **We begin to hyper-focus on things that aren't constructive**: Yes, hyper-focusing can be one of our greatest strengths. However, when our attention is focused on negative activities, like ruminating thoughts, we start to lose time and disrupt everything from our productivity to our sleep patterns. Managing hyper-focused behaviors is near impossible if we're stuck in a thought spiral that is affecting our mindset.

5. **We run the risk of developing analysis paralysis**: The term 'analysis paralysis' is when we can't make decisions or feel stuck in our own lives due to overthinking a problem. While analysis paralysis may not seem to be rooted in fear or negativity, it is often a result of us reliving our mistakes or fearing the outcome of the decisions we make.

Consequently, instead of making a decision, we begin to analyze all possible and sometimes impossible variables, being stuck in a loop of imaginable solutions rather than taking action.

Calming the ADHD brain can sometimes feel like an impossible task, especially when it is trapped in a thought spiral that threatens to consume us. Developing healthy strategies to help manage our over-thinking tendencies and make meaningful decisions for our present and future is vital to our success and mitigating the risk of developing comorbid conditions.

Strategies for Managing Your Overthinking Tendencies

You already know that overthinking is normal and that even neurotypical people will have moments when they overthink their circumstances. For the ADHD brain, changing thought processes or distracting ourselves may sometimes work, but generally speaking, snapping out of a thought spiral requires us to have solid strategies in place. When we don't manage our overthinking tendencies, we can drive ourselves into anxiety and depression, not only compounding our negative thoughts but also intensifying our other ADHD symptoms.

It's difficult for those of us with ADHD to acknowledge that most of the time, the problem isn't what *made* us ruminate but our persistence in ruminating. We must take into account that our brains have a natural tendency to hyperfixate and that certain areas of them are hardwired to be overactive or underactive. Therefore, thought spirals that aren't managed with proper strategies can really harm our mental and physical well-being.

Strategies such as stepping outside of our thoughts or challenging our feelings may work very effectively. However, the fact of the matter is that most people with ADHD simply haven't been taught how to use these strategies specifically for their minds. For example, if I told you to sit quietly and clear your mind for mindful meditation, how long would you be able to do this before fidgeting, boredom, and finally, your thoughts reentered your mind? You need to be able to take the techniques that work and apply them to your life and your unique brain so that they effectively manage your thought spirals.

Mindfulness Meditation for ADHD

For men with ADHD, internalized symptoms of boundless energy can lead to frustration and, ultimately, emotional, angry outbursts. Paying attention and practicing self-regulation can feel impossible when you need to fidget or move constantly. Self-regulating our behaviors and emotions is something we need to fine-tune and hone for the sake of our job and our relationships. Learning how to do this is one of the most invaluable tools anyone with ADHD can learn.

Most people know that mindfulness meditation is a powerful self-focus practice that has been around for centuries. Nevertheless, there are many misconceptions about the process that can turn those with ADHD away from it. The first and most common of these misconceptions is that you need to sit quietly and clear your mind in order for mindfulness meditation to work. This is simply not true!

Mindfulness meditation can be done at any time and in any quiet place for as little as five minutes, and you really don't need to clear your mind at all. The entire point of mindfulness is to observe your thoughts without judgment, letting them pass by without giving them attention or further analysis. As you begin to hone your mindfulness meditation skills, you start learning how to focus your attention on your emotional state or surroundings without feeling the need to react.

Another misconception is that you can practice mindfulness meditation a couple of times and feel a marked improvement in your ADHD symptoms. Again, this is not true because the nature of mindfulness meditation is to build a tolerance for a new behavior over time.

Think of mindfulness meditation as learning to swim. Most of us don't just jump into the deep end and expect to know how to swim like a pro. In fact, most people don't even expect to float! Like swimming, you need to wade into the shallow end and teach yourself how to focus your attention over time, eventually reaping the rewards of the practice.

Research shows that 15 minutes of mindfulness meditation per day improves mood, concentration, and emotional regulation, which contributes toward a much higher level of mental well-being (Alhawatmeh et al., 2022).

Cognitive Behavioral Therapy (CBT) to Help Curb Overthinking

CBT is an evidence-based type of psychology used to identify our negative, biased thoughts that influence our behaviors. Once a thought is identified, CBT teaches us how to reframe these thoughts and properly deal with our anxieties in a way that benefits us.

Thought spirals and overthinking are almost always based on cognitive errors, which means our spirals are caused by thoughts that are not true. Thought spirals and cognitive errors are not unique to people with ADHD; in fact, everyone has them!

The difference between a neurodiverse and a neurotypical brain is how these cognitive errors are processed. For most neurotypical people, cognitive errors will be challenged. The truth about the thought will be ascertained before disregarding the information the brain has presented the person with.

The neurodiverse brain, however, will often begin to fixate on these cognitive distortions, trying to find solutions to the false information it has provided. This creates a loop, or spiral, in which the neurodiverse person will repeatedly play the same thought scenario in their head while they try to find a solution to something that doesn't actually exist.

I'm not saying all neurotypical brains work this way. Some people will experience thought spirals without having ADHD. The issue with thought spirals is that they cause a lot of anxiety, which can develop into depression. Here's the good news, though. CBT is a proven way to help deal with these cognitive errors, breaking thought spirals and improving mood, concentration, and sleep.

The Triple-Column Method

This CBT exercise, created by David Burns, is the most effective way to challenge cognitive errors and help prevent thought spirals before they begin or stop them when they start. Studies conducted on the triple-column method show that when combined with conventional talk therapy, this exercise is extremely helpful in helping regulate emotions, manage stress, and regain control of our thought patterns (Belmont, 2017).

Of course, the first step in regaining control of your thoughts is to identify your cognitive distortions by journaling your thoughts as they happen. Any thought that isn't factually true or that you wouldn't say out loud to someone else is most likely a distortion.

There are several different kinds of cognitive distortion. Here are descriptions and examples of the most common ones:

- **All-or-nothing thinking:** Seeing things as black and white with nothing in between. *I will never be good enough.*

- **Blaming (Personalization):** Feeling responsible for everything that happens. *My colleague was rude to me today. I must have upset them somehow.*

- **Catastrophizing:** Blowing things out of proportion and thinking the worst will happen. *My boss has asked to meet with me tomorrow. I think I'm going to be in trouble and get fired.*

- **Emotional reasoning:** Believing your feelings truly relate to reality. *I feel like a total idiot, so I must be one.*

- **Fortune-telling:** Believing you can predict future outcomes. *They are offering a promotion at work. I'm sure one of my colleagues will get it instead of me.*

- **Ignoring the positive:** Focusing on any negatives in a situation, regardless of your success. *I got a thank you email from my boss today, but I bet he's sending them to everyone.*

- **Labeling:** Applying negative labels to yourself and others. *I am such an outcast here; everyone else thinks they are so amazing.*

- **Mental filter:** Picking on a negative thing and letting it affect your feelings and actions. *I know most people said my presentation was good, but I got a couple of feedback sheets that told me how to improve it, so I feel like it went really badly.*

- **Mind-reading:** Assuming you know what other people are thinking. *One of my colleagues didn't talk to me this morning. They must be upset about something.*

- **Overgeneralizing:** Taking an event and/or behavior and thinking it will happen consistently in the future. *I am always late, and I always make people angry.*

- **Shoulds & Musts:** Commanding yourself to do things. *I should be on time. I must leave the house 30 minutes earlier every day.*

Now that you know how to identify your cognitive distortion and the different types of distortion, you can create your triple-column exercise:

1. Grab a blank piece of paper, your journal, or create a new Excel spreadsheet.

2. Divide this blank page into three columns. Try to make sure you have a couple of new, pre-prepared pages so that you have your three columns handy when a thought spiral begins.

3. Label your columns as follows: column 1—Automatic thought; column 2—Distortion; and column 3—Rational response.

4. Trigger warning! Seeing your thoughts in print is often shocking and may make you sad or angry. Try to push through this stage.

5. When you have a negative thought, write it in the automatic column.

6. Now, write what the distortion is. Why is this thought untrue?

7. Next, write down the rational response to the thought.

Here's an example.

- **Automatic thought**: "I am the worst partner! My girlfriend or boyfriend hates me, and they're only with me because they feel trapped." Read your thoughts and say them out loud.

- **Distortion**: Overgeneralizing and getting into an all-or-nothing thought process. Mind-reading what my partner thinks without getting their feedback. Catastrophizing my relationship.

- **Rational response**: "I could probably do better in my relationship; everyone should try to be a better partner today than they were yesterday. My partner tells me and shows me that they love me often. There is no actual evidence that my partner wants to leave me or that they feel trapped in the relationship."

You can write down or type out as many of your automatic thoughts as you want, so don't limit yourself. At some point, your brain is going to get tired of being challenged. It will shut down your thought spiral, replacing these thoughts with confidence-boosting positive thoughts.

Like mindfulness meditation, this exercise will not work overnight; it takes time to be able to catch yourself at the beginning of the spiral and identify your distortions.

You need to become comfortable with not only recognizing when your brain is trying to hijack you, but also identifying the thoughts you are having that are exaggerated or simply not true.

If you find that you're battling to identify your thoughts or if you're becoming really frustrated with yourself during the process, take a break. Remove yourself from the situation, and take five minutes to meditate.

Like everything else in life, it takes time and practice to hone your skills, but you're at a distinct advantage, so tap into your ADHD brain's superpowers and use your tenacity and perseverance.

Part Two
Self-Regulation for Positive Transformation

Chapter 4

Your Guide to Mind Mapping

Mind mapping is a technique with several uses, including brainstorming. It doesn't require too much thought about structure and visualizes ideas so that strategies can be made to put them into action. When we are mind mapping, we essentially create a visual representation of tasks, concepts, emotions, and even the words we want to express without these elements having to be linear or organized.

In other words, mind mapping allows you to turn an abundance of thoughts into a diagram. It helps you to be organized so that you know what steps need to be taken to achieve an end goal or objective.

The best thing about mind mapping is that it is an external representation of how the human brain naturally works. This makes it perfect for people with ADHD, especially when important concepts need to be discussed or when simply creating an organized method of getting things done.

Neurodiverse and neurotypical people alike can benefit from creating mind maps as they can process information faster and recall important information much more easily than having to sift through all their daily thoughts.

In a day-to-day setting, mind mapping is used to:

• visualize concepts and brainstorm ideas

• communicate ideas so that they can be presented

- create an organizer for tasks that need completion

- run meetings in a more organic, engaging way

- summarize documentation and reports

- simplify thought processes, tasks, and projects

- communicate thoughts or emotions with more accuracy

Mind mapping is designed to help you discover what hidden strengths lie in the recesses of your subconscious mind by allowing you to put your thoughts on paper. With regular practice, it can be an incredibly powerful tool for becoming productive at work and at home. But where did the mind mapping concept originate from?

Dr. Roger Sperry, a Nobel Prize winner for his research, began studying the human brain in the early 1900s. During the course of his analysis, Sperry discovered that the cerebral cortex was divided into two hemispheres and that each hemisphere was responsible for a range of tasks.

These tasks include recognizing color, daydreaming, imagination, logic, rhythm, distinguishing lines, lists, and words, and the ability to see the bigger picture. What Sperry ascertained throughout his research was that these activities are all integrated. The higher the number of these activities being done at the same time, the more effectively the brain works to stimulate the intellect and achieve objectives.

The result of this research was mind mapping: A way in which people could exercise all of the fundamental areas of the cerebral cortex to maximize information processing and use their brain's full range of cortical abilities.

Mind mapping uses many of the functions of both the left and right hemispheres of the cerebral cortex. Therefore, people with ADHD can tap into the power of their brains to clarify, organize, and structure their thought processes without the risk of running into a negative thought spiral or bad hyperfixation.

How Mind Maps Work

Now that we know what a mind map is, we can explore how it works and why it is such a valuable way of retaining and recalling information. A mind map is the most creative and logical way of translating environmental stimuli and information into a comprehensive plan your brain can use to become more productive.

Answering the question, "How do mind maps work?" is simple. It's the creation of a detailed roadmap to where the brain stores information. Here's an example.

If a friend had moved home and you were due to visit them, they would provide you with clear, concise directions to their new home using road names and landmarks. They may even send you the coordinates of their new home so you can use GPS/ an app to show the route to your destination.

By looking at the map, you can check you're going the right way by identifying the landmarks your friend mentioned. When driving there, you will follow the directions provided by your GPS/app or by your friend to arrive at their house.

If the instructions were clear enough, using words and lines in the form of directions (left, right, and straight), and you had visual cues such as landmarks to let you know you were going in the right direction, your brain will use this information to get you to your end goal.

Mind mapping works in the same manner, and by using natural organizational structures, lines, and visual cues, your brain can be trained to reach an end goal or objective in a much easier way. Let's go back to the map example.

Over time and the more often you visit your friend, the more familiar your brain will become with recalling the landmarks and directions you initially provided it with. Eventually, you'll be able to drive to your friend's home without any instruction or active thought processes.

The end goal of mind mapping is to train your brain to filter thoughts in a way that allows you to place them on paper. Then you can use the information that is needed and disregard any that is not required. Ultimately, you will learn how to assimilate and use information quickly and without much thought.

Before I get into how to create a mind map and some techniques you can use to help you become a mind mapping ADHD master, let's look at the key elements of an effective mind map.

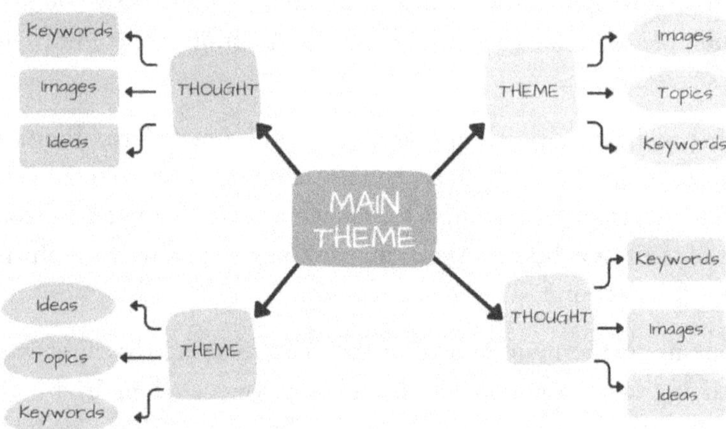

- Every mind map must have a central focus point. This can be a subject, a focus point, or a main theme. You can even use an image for this main theme if your mind works better with imagery than words.

- Lines must be used to connect themes or thoughts to the central main theme. These lines are called branches.

- Each branch must have a keyword or image placed at the end of it.

- Each branch can have topics, keywords, or images in the form of a line that is not that important to the central main theme. These lines are called twigs.

- Every branch must be relevant to and connected to the central theme, but not every twig has to connect to the central theme, only to a branch.

A Step-By-Step Guide to the Mind Mapping Process

Mind maps can be created on paper or digitally, and there are a number of great apps, which will be mentioned later, available to help people create seamless maps. Regardless of your mode of creation, mind mapping needs to follow a specific process and set of steps for it to be effective.

The Main Theme

This will be the central focus of your mind map and is the reason, purpose, or the *why* behind your map. All mind maps start from the middle and branch outward, so the central idea must be the core topic of your map.

Here are some ideas for why you might want to create a mind map:

• You're facing an obstacle or challenge that you're unable to work through, e.g., you want to find a new job.

• You're brainstorming ways in which you can become more organized and productive at work.

• You're battling to grasp a difficult concept or idea.

• You're trying to simplify a complex idea or piece of information.

• You're trying to break through a creative block.

• You would like to express complex emotions or feelings.

• You would like to set attainable goals for yourself.

Add Your Branches

Once you have your central theme, you can begin your map by adding branches to cover subtopics. These branches don't need to be organized in any way, shape, or form and shouldn't contain much information. Keywords and short phrases are more than enough information for you to create a proper branch.

If your mind wanders while you are creating your branches, add a twig and place this information on the twig if it doesn't deserve its own branch. These branches will be the source of information for your center point.

Add Twigs

Once you have branches attached to your main theme, you can begin to add twigs to each branch. The only rule with twigs is to ensure the information you are adding is relevant to the branch. If it isn't, then it shouldn't be on your mind map, and you can disregard the thought.

There is absolutely no limit to the number of branches or twigs you can add to your mind map. Thus, let your brain wander, and see how many thoughts and ideas you can come up with that pertain to your central theme.

Add Some Colors and Images

Just like your roadmap to your friend's house, the information on your mind map will be better stored and more effective if you add landmarks or visual representations of where you should be in your journey.

Adding colors, shapes, and images will also ensure you are engaging both lobes of your cerebral cortex, thereby maximizing your brain's ability to process and store information. The more areas of your brain you use when creating your mind map, the more likely your brain will be to retain the information and recall it later on.

Here is a working example of a mind map when planning how to find a job. This main theme is placed in the center.

Branching off from the main theme are four topics that are steps in the process of finding a job. Moving around the map in a clockwise direction, starting with the top left box, these are: write a resume and cover letter; do a job search; apply for jobs, and prepare for interviews.

These branches then separate off into twigs that show the relevant and connected tasks that need to be done. For example, when writing a resume and cover letter, it is worth doing some online research and looking at templates. You may know other people who have recently done this, so you can get some advice, and when you have completed these documents, you can ask them to check for any mistakes or missing information.

Mind Mapping Techniques for Men With ADHD

The world of business has never moved faster than it does today, and ADHD can sometimes be a distinct disadvantage for men in the workplace. Disorganization, procrastination, and taking longer to do tasks can all hinder productivity within the workplace. This can subsequently lead to feelings of inadequacy, frustration, and sometimes disciplinary action from management for not completing tasks. For men with ADHD, job satisfaction and a work-life balance can be challenging as productivity slips and personal relationships begin to suffer due to pent-up energy and stress.

Both partners in a relationship generally work, so they are expected to assist with household tasks to help split the mental and physical load within the home. Mind mapping offers men in the workplace a unique opportunity to organize their home and career spaces, becoming more organized and efficient with the tasks that need to be done in both places.

All of this leads to a greater sense of accomplishment, self-confidence, and the ability to shine in professional and personal roles. While the basics of mind mapping remain the same, the techniques of mind mapping for men with ADHD may require some tweaking for the tool to be completely effective.

The reason for this is that most adult men with ADHD have a lifetime of dysfunctional habits they have learned. While these habits can be unlearned, it takes time, effort, and the right tools, plus the ability to be productive and efficient in the moment.

With all of this in mind, it's important to remember that the basics of mind mapping will remain the same. There must be a main theme in the center of the page. Branches come from it with ideas, information, or interconnected concepts, and wings break off into additional ideas. Each of these ideas must be interrelated; if other themes crop up, a separate mind map can be created for each of them.

The difference between standard or neurotypical mind maps and ADHD mind maps is simplifying or disseminating the information on the mind map. As the ADHD brain is generally far "busier" than the typical one and because some irrelevant information may be transferred onto a mind map, it's essential to refine it.

Additionally, a mind map should be used to create a concise list of milestones or objectives that break tasks down into smaller, more manageable ones to achieve a greater goal.

Here's how to refine your mind map:

• Identify your central theme as usual.

• Add details in the form of branches and twigs, as usual.

• Look for relationships between your central theme and your branches and twigs.

• Separate these relationships by color. Choose your own colors or use red for branch themes, black for dates, blue for explanations, green for facts, and another color for additional information.

• Once you have your twigs and branches color-organized, begin looking for your organizing principle. This principle is the logical sequence in which your tasks should be done. For example, you wouldn't hand in a task you haven't completed yet, or put the vacuum cleaner away if you haven't yet vacuumed the house. This step may take some time when you first start mind mapping, but it will get easier with time.

• Move your tasks around in chronological or logical order. Place your central theme at the top of your list. Use your colors to discern whether your tasks are, in fact, in the right order. Run this order through your mind or say it out loud so that you can double-check that it makes sense.

Any branches or twigs that are not yet on your chronological list will need to be checked to see whether they need to be a part of your process. Slot them into your list where they need to go or discard them if they are not required.

• Finally, redraw your map with your items in chronological order. In this final draft, look for ways to make your objectives and milestones stand out. Use colorful borders, images, or other visual reminders to help prompt you with the next steps you should take.

• Put your finalized mind map up where you can see it and consult it when you need to do a task. Once you have completed a task or an objective, be sure to tick it off your map and celebrate your victory in achieving this milestone.

You should find a non-material way to reward yourself whenever you get a task done or complete one of your objectives. It is a critical step in creating new habits to replace your dysfunctional ones. This is because habits are formed in a loop that involves a routine, a cue, and a reward. In creating your own routine, cue, and reward cycle, you'll be effectively developing a habit loop that benefits your life and well-being.

Mind Mapping Tools and Technology

One of the greatest things about living in a modern technological era is that technology can help us simplify, organize, and visualize our thoughts and ideas, allowing us to have a clear mind map to success. Mind mapping tools and software enable us to give structure and order to our complex ideas, connecting all the steps we need to take to achieve a goal.

Mind mapping software is an amazing way to simplify the process of creating a mind map for whatever purpose you need. This may include making changes to your personal life, bringing your vision boards to life, and becoming more productive at work.

The benefits of using mind mapping tools and technology include:

• The simplification of your mind mapping process and creation: Mind mapping software and tools allow you to create a comprehensive list of ideas and thoughts in one space that color codes your projects as you develop. Modifications to this thought process don't require you to create a whole new mind map, as changes can be easily applied digitally.

• The ability to collaborate with other team or family members: Collaboration ensures you are not working at cross-purposes with the people in your life. Collaborative maps that allow invited members to contribute their ideas are extremely helpful in creating behaviors that facilitate great interpersonal relationships.

• The integration of other apps: Being able to integrate other apps into your mind mapping process is incredibly valuable, especially in the early phases when you may need reminders to begin tasks. Integration with programs such as Google Workspaces, calendars, and Microsoft Teams means you'll never miss a reminder or opportunity to share your progress and the planning of your day, as well as facilitate great collaboration.

• Software creates mind maps that are easy to follow: While traditional mind maps are great, their format may not work with each unique brain. Using mind mapping tools and technology will give you a choice of how you want your map to be displayed. You can select the way that best resonates with your brain, creating an effective memory jog and call to action. In addition, mind mapping tools will allow you to add different elements to your map, and you can customize everything from your line styling to your colors and even your branch and twig positioning.

Now that you know the advantages of using mind mapping tools and technology, you can begin to explore the various options available to you.

Suggested Mind Mapping Technologies

Below is a list of some of the more popular mind mapping tools available across different platforms. This is by no means an extensive list, and a quick Google search will provide you with many tools for your specific mind mapping purpose:

• **MindGenius**: A simple-to-use tool that includes customizable backgrounds, branch shapes and fills, and custom task boards that allow you to track your milestones.

• **MindMeister**: A great collaborative mind map that lets you share your ideas, milestones, and goals with other people. The app is cross-platform, which means it can be used and accessed across browsers and devices such as Android and iOS.

• **Xmind**: Features minimalist interfaces and simplistic charts and layouts for people who don't like busy mind maps. Each layout is customizable, and the software includes logic charts, brace maps, tree charts, timelines, etc. The software is cross-platform for browsers on Android and iOS.

- **SimpleMind**: For people who are not technologically advanced, SimpleMind is straightforward and easy to use. It offers different templates and forms of mind mapping that include monthly planners, flowcharts, and organizational charts.

These are only suggestions for the different software options available to you. It's up to you to find a mind mapping tool that works best for you and your specific needs. Remember, everyone's brain works uniquely, and this means different tools and software will not resonate the same way for everyone.

Incorporating Mind Mapping for Workplace Productivity

You now know that mind mapping can be an incredibly effective tool for helping you build your organizational skills and become more productive. Since men with ADHD often face battles in the workplace, mind mapping can be used as a way to become a valuable member of your company's team. Mind mapping in the workplace can range from creating basic maps to using more complex and specific forms of tools that can help build and maintain focus.

The most common of these mind maps are listed below. Have a look at each of these, do some further research, and try to use whichever applies to your role or position in your company.

Flowcharts

The most basic form of mind mapping in any organization is done with flowcharts. They use mapping symbols and illustrations to display the inputs and outputs of a process, plus each specific step and milestone required to achieve a goal.

Basic flowcharts are usually used to plan projects, document processes, improve communication, brainstorm solutions, and manage workflows. Flowcharts are the best tool to show how a project will progress from start to finish.

High-Level Process Maps

These mind maps show a process from the top down, which gives a much higher-level view of a goal. These mind maps only show the essential steps in achieving a goal and, as such, contain only minimal details.

Generally speaking, high-level process maps are solely used to define business processes and identify the key areas required to achieve success. High-level process maps are used to illustrate and discuss processes with a third party that isn't actively involved in a specific project.

Detailed Process Map

Detailed process maps are the exact opposite of high-level process maps and specify each process and sub-process required to complete a task. The hallmark of this type of mind map is that it documents each decision point as well as the inputs and outputs needed for each step of a project. Detailed process maps are the most effective way to create a visual understanding of complex tasks, identifying areas of possible inefficiency and how to overcome them. Detailed process maps are best used to develop an understanding of a process and to list contingency plans.

Swimlane Map

This mind map is cross-functional and is sometimes called a deployment flowchart. The goal of a swimlane map is to designate certain activities for people. Each of these activities is situated in a swimlane.

Every swimlane is assigned to a specific stakeholder who will be responsible for the activities within that channel. As such, swimlane maps are great for new employees who don't know their roles or processes properly yet, or to increase accountability within a team.

Value Stream Map

This type of mind map is primarily used as a lean management tool that assists in the visualization of the processes required to create a product or service. Value stream maps are very complex, using specific symbols rather than words to help illustrate the flow of the processes as well as any materials required.

While documenting this data may not seem like a big deal, value stream data allows teams and external stakeholders to identify when products and materials need to be delivered. This saves valuable time during a project as less time is focused on what is happening or needs to be acquired next. It allows each person to focus on what is required of them right now.

As such, value stream maps are best for highlighting the processes involved in developing a product or service and documenting each process with quantitative data.

SIPOC Diagram or Map

SIPOC stands for suppliers, inputs, processes, outputs, and customers. While SIPOC diagrams are not really maps, they do chart certain elements of a process that are key to success. Usually, SIPOC diagrams are used as a precursory step in drafting a more detailed process map for a team or individual.

SIPOC diagrams are presented with a minimum of five columns. In each of these columns, the processes, outputs, and inputs of the process are highlighted, as well as any other pertinent information.

This type of map is used to prepare detailed process maps by defining the scope of more detailed or complex processes. It also identifies key elements and the stakeholders involved in a process from start to finish.

Symbols You May Need to Know

Mind maps that are used in the workplace will often come with specific symbols. These symbols are called Unified Modeling Language

(UML), and each of them represents the elements of a process, including inputs, outputs, steps, decision points, and stakeholders.

Each organization that uses mind maps will train its team members in this language and the symbols associated with it. In the meantime, here is a list so that you can begin your corporate mind mapping journey:

- **Oval:** Denotes a terminator, which is the beginning or end of a process.

- **Rectangle:** Denotes a step, activity, or task involved in the process.

- **Arrow:** Denotes the directional flow of the steps in the process.

- **Diamond:** Denotes a decision and will be displayed when a critical decision needs to be made. These will be answered yes or no, and branches will be given for both responses.

- **D:** Denotes a delay.

- **Parallelogram:** Denotes data that is part of the input or output of the process.

- **Rectangle with a slanted top:** Denotes data that needs to be manually entered.

- **Rectangle with double vertical lines:** Denotes a subprocess that doesn't necessarily directly pertain to the project but is needed.

Tracking Your Progress and Achievements

Once you have created your mind map, the next phase is to institute the steps you have created for yourself. Actioning your mind map will ensure you are making steady progress toward achieving your goals. Plus, it's also important to actively track your progress so you can celebrate your successes and achievements.

Before reading the steps below, I'd like you to know that there is no metric or measure for success because everyone's definition of success is different. Getting up in the morning, leaving your home neat and tidy after doing five minutes of mindfulness meditation, and arriving on time wherever you're going is a success.

Successes and achievements can sometimes be the minuscule things we do that facilitate a better life, great habits, and overall well-being. You simply cannot impose someone else's definition of success on yourself. You can absolutely look to others for inspiration and ideas but always remember that this is your life, which means applying the things that are important to you.

Take the time to define success for yourself and decide what small changes you need to make so that you can ultimately reach your end goal. Now that you know what success looks like for you and what you'd like to improve and work toward, let's get down to how you can track your progress.

• Break your achievement goal into milestones. You may know what you want to achieve, but you'll need to create steps for how to get there. Mind mapping allows you to create these milestones so you can list them in order of priority. The goal here is not to change everything at once but one small thing at a time.

• Set deadlines for your milestones, not your goal. It's best not to set a deadline for your actual goal but rather to set completion dates for each milestone, deciding when you will have accomplished or instituted each of them. In setting timeframes for your milestones, you are not overwhelming yourself with the bigger picture. It's the old analogy of how to eat an elephant ... one bite at a time.

• Tick off your milestones and celebrate them! That's right; you need to focus on rewarding yourself for the small actions and steps you're taking. This is because your goal will be self-rewarding, but if you don't celebrate each milestone achieved, it's going to begin to feel like you're running a never-ending marathon. Celebrate all of your success, but more specifically, celebrate your consistent improvements.

• Consider turning your mind map into specific, measurable, achievable, relevant, time-based goals (SMART). There is a reason SMART goals work: they're broken down into smaller milestones with deadlines that can be monitored and tracked with precision. SMART goals automatically create a map that is specific, measures your progress, and ensures you can move toward your end goal in a sustainable way.

• Review where you were and where you are. A great way to celebrate your small victories is to look back and see how much you have progressed over a short period of time. Reviewing your progress and even documenting it if you like will help you remain motivated when it feels a little overwhelming or like you're not doing enough to progress. It's normal to beat yourself up on bad days, but it's also important that, in those moments, you acknowledge your progress too.

If you feel like you're losing track of your progress or have lost sight of the bigger picture altogether, you're not alone. Many people come across obstacles as they put their mind maps into practice.

Some of these common obstacles include:

• Fixating on the details rather than taking action.

• Getting too involved in the type or aesthetic of the mind map.

• Not organizing the information gathered from the mind map.

• Not combining your mind maps to ascertain common goals or purposes.

• Not using images and colors that resonate with you or only using words.

• Not summarizing your thought processes or being too long-winded with your map.

Always remember that your mind map is a way to focus your thoughts into a clear, concise plan that should be used to improve your life and achieve your goals.

Be thoughtful in the creation of your mind map, avoid common mistakes, and understand that the definition of success is extremely personal. This will help you take the steps you need to take in your own journey to achieving your goals.

Chapter 5

Executive Functioning 101

Executive function skills and the ability to self-regulate go hand-in-hand. Without executive functioning, we are unable to remain focused, follow instructions, or complete multi-step tasks effectively. Consequently, if we do not learn executive functioning, our brain cannot prioritize tasks, control our impulses, set or achieve goals, or filter out environmental distractions.

Human beings are not born with executive function skills. They are developed throughout childhood and adolescence via exposure to other people, correction, and life experiences.

Children and adults with executive dysfunction can struggle in life as the positive behaviors expected of them to integrate into society and make good choices are lacking.

Additionally, children who don't learn executive functioning skills also lack self-regulation, memory, mental flexibility, and self-control skills. Therefore, they experience more challenges than typical children.

While this may not sound like a major problem, the reality is that executive function skills are highly interrelated with other neural functions, including working memory, mental flexibility, and the ability to control impulses.

It's important to note that although no one is born with executive functioning skills, everyone has the ability to develop them. Children with neurodiverse brains may just require a little extra support in developing these skills. Sadly, most children with ADHD are not afforded this support because neurotypical adults find ADHD difficult to manage.

They are placed in traditional classrooms, where teachers are often assigned more students than they can cope with; therefore, children with ADHD do not receive individual attention for developing these skills. This creates a compounded issue in which children grow up without the very skills they need to belong in society.

While more attention has been brought to ADHD as a real behavioral condition in modern society, entire generations have grown up without these critical skills, creating a group of adults who are seriously struggling through life.

Children and adults with ADHD need to be in environments that promote growth. They need to practice these critical skills safely so they can begin to establish the right routines and start to model good social behaviors.

Developing an understanding of executive functioning, practicing the required skills, and learning to manage stress effectively all contribute toward fast-tracking proper neural function.

A Deeper Understanding of Executive Functioning Skills

Executive functioning is a set of skills that include your memory, the ability to control your impulses, and being flexible in your thinking. These skills are used every day of our lives to manage tasks at work and at home, to create a sense of belonging in society, and to regulate our emotions.

With executive dysfunction, it can become very difficult to follow instructions, focus on anything, recall memories or information, and regulate your emotions effectively. All of this contributes to stress, lowered self-esteem, and a feeling that you don't belong in society.

While I have briefly explained what executive function is, it is important that you have a deeper understanding of it and how it directly affects your life. This understanding will serve as your purpose or the *why* behind learning these critical skills, and will be addressed in a later chapter.

A great way to think of your brain is that it's a busy international airport. There are multiple flights landing and taking off 24 hours a day, passengers rushing to get to their gate or to be picked up, people sitting about in restaurants, and others trying to catch up on their work tasks for the day.

Without air traffic control, information desks, and proper signage, the airport would be chaotic. No one would know what was expected of them, where they should go, or when they were expected to get onto a plane that may or may not be able to take off or land safely.

Airports need management systems for them to run safely and correctly, and so does your brain. This neural management system is executive function, and it ensures working memory, cognitive flexibility, and inhibitory control are in place.

Without executive function skills, attention span, organization, planning, prioritizing, task completion, the ability to see different points of view, emotional regulation, and self-monitoring are all lacking. Neurotypical brains will learn executive functioning skills as a part of the normal social correction process, but they can continue to develop well into a person's 20s. A lack of special attention to these skills in neurodiverse people can mean they lag behind their typical peers and, as a result, have more challenges when they are adults.

Some of the primary signs that you are a neurodiverse person who is lacking in executive skills include:

• Struggling to begin or complete tasks.

• An inability or battle to prioritize tasks.

• Having poor short-term memory or forgetting things you've heard or read.

- Struggling to follow sequential steps or directions.

- Needing a routine or panicking when a routine is changed.

- Struggling to switch focus from one thing to the next.

- Becoming fixated on things.

- Having an emotional response to situations or struggles that are not a big deal.

- Struggling to focus or organize thoughts.

- An inability to manage time.

An ADHD diagnosis means that there is an executive function issue, but when these critical skills are not developed, other comorbid conditions like learning disabilities can arise. Having said that, people can have executive functioning issues without having ADHD, and people can think differently or struggle with certain aspects of these skills without having any disorders. Not having the right grounding in executive functioning skills does not mean a person is stupid, lazy, or belligerent.

What Causes Executive Dysfunction?

Research into what causes executive function issues is still pretty new, but preliminary findings suggest there are two main contributing factors. When reading this section, you should keep in mind that people with ADHD will always have some level of executive dysfunction, especially if special attention and skills-building have not been a part of their treatment plan.

The reason people with ADHD have executive dysfunction is rooted in neural differences. Men with ADHD are more likely to carry executive dysfunction into adulthood because hyperactive behaviors and a lack of concentration are labeled as hallmark male traits.

The two main reasons for executive dysfunction are:

1. A brain that is neurodiverse, which causes certain areas of the brain to be under or overactive.

Certain areas of the ADHD brain develop differently from neurotypical ones, and the ones used for executive skills like memory and emotional centers may evolve more slowly.

While science is not sure why this happens, genetics may play a role, and people with executive dysfunction may find that family members suffer from these dysfunctions too.

2. Environmental factors may contribute to executive dysfunction. These may include having a parent with executive dysfunction, not having a proper emotional attachment to parents, abuse, economic hardship, neglectful caregiving, and chaotic home environments.

Some studies suggest a third possible cause is that learning disorders may be a factor in executing functional challenges. Having said that, research has neither proved nor disproved this, so these findings are purely opinion-based at this stage.

Executive Dysfunction Diagnosis

There are no official diagnostic criteria for executive function challenges. Regardless, during the review and assessment process for an ADHD diagnosis, executive function will be assessed.

Some of these assessment criteria will include:

• the ability to maintain attention

• inhibitory control

• issues with short-term memory or working memory

• issues with planning or organization

• concept formation issues

• inability to move from one task to another easily

• word and idea generation issues

Testing for executive functioning challenges will almost always be done as part of a full evaluation for other comorbid conditions. It's important to go to a licensed, registered mental health professional like a psychologist or psychiatrist when testing executive functioning.

Boosting Executive Functioning

People with ADHD have issues with focusing their attention, hyperactivity, and impulse control, which can lead to executive dysfunction. Deficits in executive function can lead to a lowered sense of well-being and cause practical issues in a person's professional and personal life.

Because everything from cognitive skills to planning and prioritizing is affected by executive dysfunction, other comorbid conditions can begin to surface, and the most common of these are anxiety and depression.

For people who are medicated for their ADHD, executive functioning does not improve. Studies show that as many as 80% of people who are medicated for their ADHD will have no improvement in their ability to focus, short-term memory function, or distractibility without actively working on these skills (Roth & Saykin, 2004).

Medicating ADHD without addressing or correcting the behaviors associated with the condition and without teaching the skills required to improve executive function is like placing a bandage on an infected wound.

Issues need to be addressed from the inside out so that new neural pathways can be formed and the development of good habits can begin. In his Psychology Today blog, Scott S. Shapiro, M.D. describes five strategies that can be used to help improve executive function skills in relation to adult ADHD and work.

Step 1: Clarify Expectations

The first step in developing executive function is to clarify what needs to be done, how it should be done, and by when. Men with ADHD are often extremely enthusiastic about setting and achieving goals but lose momentum quickly. The reason for this is that goals and expectations are often not well-thought-out or time-bound and lack clear direction.

Having clear expectations often goes beyond personal goal-setting. In a workplace where the ADHD man is expected to perform well and achieve milestones, not having clarity can lead to hyperfixation or confusion. The ADHD man's enthusiasm for tasks, while helpful, tends to stall achieving goals as they don't have an understanding of or clarity on the steps required to complete these milestones and goals. To negate this issue, it's important that questions are asked and the answers are written down.

Here are some questions you can ask to help guide you in setting expectations.

1. What is the goal, and what does success specifically look like?
2. What is the time frame for each milestone required for success?
3. What is the scope of this project?
4. What specific details should be paid attention to for this project to be a success?

It's important to ask as many questions as you can to gain clarity on what is expected of you.

Step 2: Request Feedback

Men with ADHD can tend to view failure as something fatal or a reflection of their character. These thought distortions often stem from early childhood when their behavior provoked angry responses from adults or other kids ostracized them. Thought distortions can instill a deep sense of self-doubt, shame, and avoidance of doing tasks for fear of failing or making a mistake.

Asking for regular feedback or creating a positive feedback loop is a great way to know that you are on track with a project and meeting all the required expectations.

Organizations will often insist that leaders meet with their staff on a monthly basis. However, more regular feedback meetings are hugely beneficial to people with ADHD so they can remain on track with their assigned tasks.

Meeting frequently with leaders and stakeholders also instills a sense of accountability and improves motivation. It also allows changes to be made during the process rather than waiting until the end of a project when issues may become overwhelming or irreversible.

Step 3: Write Out Strategies

The nature of modern workplaces is that teams often undertake large projects, so every team member must pull their weight to complete the project successfully. This can potentially cause issues when strategies and expectations are not clear, which can lead to people with ADHD feeling isolated or that they have let other people down.

An easy way to overcome this is to make sure strategies are written out in a simplified format, showing each milestone and the steps that need to be taken to achieve them.

Mind mapping is a great way to do this, as it enables men with ADHD to visualize a project properly and effectively without becoming overwhelmed with everything that needs to be done.

There are other ways to write out projects in the form of flowcharts, as discussed in the previous chapter, and the simple steps that can be taken to achieve an end goal. The ADHD brain works best when it is offered a combination of visual and physical stimuli, which is why handwritten strategies are preferred over typed-out ones. Studies show that writing notes activates more areas of the brain and leads to better recall of the information.

If you would prefer to use an app, that's fine, but do write out your strategy before transferring it to your app. Handwritten strategies don't need to be super precise or perfect by any means, but they should anticipate all of the steps required or the questions that need to be asked to remain on track with a goal.

Step 4: Add Tasks and Milestones to a Calendar

For most people, calendars with proper reminder notifications are useful, but for the ADHD brain, they're a necessity. Most men who have overcome executive function issues will tell you, "If it's not documented with reminders set, it simply doesn't exist!" When critical tasks are not recorded in a diary or added to a calendar, there is a big chance that they will be forgotten about or fall through the cracks.

This means listing all of the steps of a project with their deadline dates and setting reminders that allow adequate time to get the milestones done. When adding reminders, you're ensuring nothing slips by unnoticed and putting a contingency in place that helps you stay informed about upcoming tasks. It's a good idea to both write these steps out on paper and add them to an electronic calendar so that visual and kinetic stimuli come into play.

Step 5: Create an Organizer's Handbook

Men with ADHD can sometimes be oblivious to socially acceptable behavior or the rules of engagement in an organizational setting. This is by no means intentional, but once awareness is brought to this conflicting behavior, it should be changed quickly to prevent social isolation.

Creating an organizer handbook filled with the rules, regulations, and expectations required to be a functional member of any team is the perfect ADHD tool for building executive skills.

This handbook can contain information on people that will help you bond with them. You can log anything outside of project scopes that need to be done by you, organizational requirements or rules you tend to forget, and feedback you have received that will help you improve. Think of your handbook as a "master guide."

Having this kind of instruction manual allows you to enter social and professional situations armed with knowledge. It removes the fear associated with feeling or acting differently or letting people down.

Time Management Strategies for Men With ADHD

The restless and impulsive nature of people with ADHD can create time blindness because they think of time differently than neurotypical people. These time perception differences can also mean people with ADHD have issues estimating how long tasks will take, how much time needs to be spent on each milestone, and when tasks should be done.

Research has shown that ADHD distorts time in the brain because it requires a number of sections, including the prefrontal cortex, anterior cingulate, and supplementary motor area (Weissenberger et al., 2021).

This means deadlines and showing up on time are a real struggle for people with ADHD. However, procrastination, improper planning, and becoming distracted easily are all manageable symptoms.

Take a look at the strategies below. While they all work, it's up to you to try each of them and implement the ones that help you manage your time more effectively.

Externalize Your Time

People with ADHD can struggle to understand time as a whole concept, so it's important that you question time to gain proper clarity.

Questions like:

- What is this due, and by when?

- How long should this task take? Can you please be specific about a date and time?

- How well have I managed my time so far?

Asking questions like these helps supplement the brain's internal ability to process time, but these internal reminders may be forgotten without externalized tools like clocks, calendars, or audible reminders.

For the ADHD brain, analog clocks are best to help process time properly, and they can help the brain become consciously aware of the passage of time. Successfully managing time begins with awareness of time and intentionally acting within prespecified boundaries.

In other words, even if you're aware of what the time is and you can see the clock moving, the chances are you won't pay attention to it unless you have a reminder or alarm that pushes you to take action.

If you are one of those people who is a stickler for details or are stuck in a rut of procrastination, setting high-priority reminders will help you take action more effectively. Proactive time management ensures you will be able to complete more tasks and accomplish more during the day. Nevertheless, you should be aware of overfilling your schedule with too much in a day.

It's normal to become enthusiastic about your newfound time management skills, but it's important that you don't overdo it. Block out your time and ensure you prioritize the tasks that have to be done before the things you *want* to do.

Practice Essentialism

American author and business strategist Greg McKeown coined the term 'essentialism' as a way to decide in what areas a person would like to succeed in their lives. The reality is that everyone can't be good at everything all the time, nor do they have to be. By stopping trying to do everything and focusing on what is essential, people can achieve their goals faster and contribute more to the world.

To implement an essentialist lifestyle, you need to define what it means to succeed and, more specifically, what success means to you. That way, you can deliberately allocate your precious time and energy to the things that matter. When you are in control and can choose the things that are important to you, you're creating value and reward in your actions.

Considering your strengths, decide what tasks have to be prioritized, including those chores we all hate doing if they cannot be delegated to someone else. Then make a list of the things that are important to you and that you believe will bring value to your life. Use these things as a way to experiment with your time management and be progressive in taking the right action to achieve your goals.

Learn to Time Block

Looking at the bigger picture and seeing everything that needs to be done can feel overwhelming. Time blocking allows you to focus your attention on one chunk of a task at a time, with the understanding that completing smaller quantities of a task will get everything done on time. For example, you might block out two 30-minute time slots in your calendar each day to respond to emails rather than being distracted by them as they arrive.

Time blocking also lets you celebrate the smaller milestones you have accomplished, leading to higher motivation toward completing the full task. How you block out your time is entirely up to you, and the only prerequisite to time-blocking is to ensure that critical or priority tasks are completed first. In Chapter 7, there is a practical exercise to do to get you started.

Keep To-Do Lists Updated

A master list is an amazing organizational tool, but it can all amount to nothing if you are not keeping your lists up-to-date and crossing off completed items.

Having a to-do list is also a great way to preserve your energy and attention because you're not trying to remember all the important things that need to be done on a day-to-day basis.

With any to-do list, consistency is key, and if you are one of those people who has a lot to do, create more than one master list so that the crucial tasks for the day in each category can be tackled first.

Having more than one master list will also show you whether or not you've overcommitted yourself and allow you the opportunity to delegate tasks that are not critical for you to do.

Finally, don't get too caught up in things you shouldn't be doing. Instead, focus on what *must* be done and then tackle the items you want to do once these critical tasks are complete.

Make Use of Tech

Technology can serve as one of our greatest distractions or one of the most effective tools we own to help manage our time. Every smartphone can be used to set reminders, create task lists, and have a calendar with notification functions. Visual and audio reminders are an amazing way to help keep you aware of the time and when to shift to the next task.

To find out about the best 5 apps to help with your ADHD, download your free bonus!

https://selftransformationpath.com/BundlePB
You can also scan this QR code to get access.

Analyze Your Brain's Patterns

Everyone has times when they are most productive or when it feels like everything works seamlessly. Conversely, there are certain periods of the day when we can become unproductive for no particular reason. If we're not careful about managing them, these unproductive times can threaten to derail our entire day.

Analyzing your brain's productivity patterns will allow you to schedule your concentration-intense tasks during your effective times and use your less productive periods to complete tasks that don't require your full attention.

Rather than focusing on the periods you are battling to concentrate or beating yourself up about struggling through tasks, reshuffle your day and time-blocked segments to help your brain work when it's at its optimum.

The more you analyze your brain's patterns throughout the day, the more opportunity you give yourself to work efficiently and productively. In addition, by allowing your brain time to rest while still being productive on non-intensive tasks when concentration levels are low, you're building a sense of achievement *and* ticking things off your to-do list.

Create Routines Around Your Patterns

The brain remembers things more easily when it has a routine because routines are patterns too. In fact, your brain will respond to these routines better if you split them into daytime and nighttime routines.

The trick to creating a routine is to work around patterns you have already formed for your life. For example, if you brush your teeth after drinking your coffee in the morning and take your medication while you pick up your car keys, it's important that you don't disrupt this pattern. Instead, you could add something to your routine in slow or "dead" moments. What do I mean?

Let's say you have ten free minutes between drinking your coffee and brushing your teeth. You fill this time with scrolling social media before heading to the bathroom to continue your routine.

If you broke these ten minutes in half, you would have five minutes to practice mindfulness meditation and five minutes to scroll social media without disrupting your routine. In fact, you would've created a pattern within a pattern if you consistently practiced your mindfulness meditation every morning, building upon your habitual patterns.

Routines developed around our brain's patterns help us function more efficiently and ensure we're not wasting time, which ultimately makes us feel terrible. Analyzing our behavioral patterns also allows us to see how much time we're spending doing things that are not healthy or productive for us so that we can make better choices.

Gift Yourself Time

Ask anyone with ADHD what causes them anxiety, and somewhere on their list will be rushing from one thing to the next. Rushing around or knowing that you're going to be late or won't have enough time to complete a task will cause you to feel stressed out, even if you aren't consciously aware of your stress.

This anxiety and being late for things are inevitable, especially when your brain simply doesn't perceive time in the same way as a neurotypical one. A fantastic way to overcome this issue is to gift yourself time by allowing yourself a grace period between tasks or when having to leave to go somewhere.

Instead of setting your reminder or alarm to leave or stop what you're doing immediately, set two reminders, one to let you know it's time to wind down or get ready and another to let you know it's time to go or begin your next task.

In addition, it's a good idea to give yourself a break between tasks where you get up, stretch, grab something to eat, or just walk around a little bit. What is important during these breaks is not to start anything new or begin social media scrolling on your phone.

Create Realistic Estimations of Time

One of the biggest challenges people with ADHD face is not that they're lazy; it's that they take on too much at once. An all-or-nothing mindset can cause serious panic and ultimately set you up for failure. While blocking out your time will definitely help you see what a realistic amount of work is, it's still essential to estimate the amount of time you will need to do something. This means factoring in unforeseen events, like your laptop needing an update, as well as being realistic about how long a task will take.

For people with ADHD, estimating time can be difficult, and the best way to overcome this challenge is to time yourself doing tasks. Once you have completed them several times, you'll be able to ascertain an average and add your time buffer to this average timeframe.

Change Your Perspective and Expectations

It's important to change your perspective about time and your expectations of how much you can do with your time. Whether you're in the midst of a time crisis or simply don't know how to manage your time effectively, changing your perspective will allow you to take a deep breath and reframe the situation.

Changing your perspective can be done by:

• Slowing things down and allowing yourself to stop panicking or feeling anxious about time.

• Delegating tasks that are not essential for you to do.

• Recalling a time when you could gain control of your time.

• Working things backward rather than forward, from your goal to your milestones, so that you can allocate enough time to tasks.

• Rewarding yourself for tasks that are completed.

• Setting time limits for social media.

Finally, I'd like you to know that even neurotypical people have issues with time. In fact, men, in general, find time management and tasks that require multiple steps or task-switching challenging.

This is because boys are not taught these skills when they are younger because of societal gender roles and stereotypes. Not being taught these skills instills certain behaviors in boys that are often carried through into adulthood. The good news is that behaviors can be changed, and you have the power to reclaim your time management skills.

A Word on Being Organized

Being organized with your time and space is the key to becoming efficiently productive. Remember, being organized doesn't mean having a meticulously clean space; it simply means finding a system that works for you.

When you create an organized environment, you spend less time looking for things and more time completing the tasks required to be productive and achieve your goals.

This is what an organization can look like:

• keeping track of your progress

• using calendars and mind maps efficiently

• creating to-do lists and keeping them up-to-date

• being accountable for your actions and changing negative behaviors

• actively eliminating distractions

• using timers and reminders

• maintaining a clean environment

• using labels to find things easily

• placing tasks, like emails, in digital folders and clearing out things that have already been done

• taking sufficient breaks between tasks

• setting SMART goals

Goal Setting for Men With ADHD

ADHD is something you're going to have for your entire life. For you to truly unlock your ADHD superpowers, you're going to need to work toward your strengths, setting goals that will help you develop and grow throughout your entire adult life.

As mentioned in Chapter 4, setting SMART goals is still the most effective way to achieve what you want to achieve in life. However, it's critical that you back these goals up with action, and this is where the ADHD brain can sometimes derail your plans.

There are six superpower skills you can use to empower yourself to take action and achieve your goals:

Skill 1: Focus on Your Strengths

It's important that you focus on your strengths and not your weaknesses. This doesn't mean you can't work on your weaknesses; it simply means you shouldn't focus on the things you believe you can't do.

Negative belief systems can cause issues for you, adversely affect your behaviors, and make you feel terrible about yourself. Focusing on the positive, however, will ensure you're celebrating all of the things you can do.

Skill 2: Make Your Goals Your Own

If you're working toward someone else's goals, you're not going to see the value in them when they're achieved. You need to take the time to define what success means to you so that you can set goals that have a purpose for *your* life. These goals can be broken down into different life areas, including your hobbies, health, fitness, career, etc.

Skill 3: Have Milestones

Part of setting SMART goals is creating milestones, but even these can overwhelm the ADHD brain. Make sure that when you set goals, you are time-blocking your milestones, organizing them into a group of manageable tasks per time slot.

You can ask yourself the following questions when setting milestones:

• What is the shortest amount of time I need to achieve this milestone?

- How many milestones are needed to achieve my goal?

- What can I do when I feel overwhelmed or procrastinate?

- If I do this task now, how much closer am I to my goal?

Skill 4: Learn Self-Discipline, Not Motivation

Motivation is a temporary emotion, which is why so many people start a goal and never achieve it. When setting goals, you're also going to need to determine how you're going to build self-discipline so that you continue achieving milestones and reach your ultimate goal.

Without self-discipline, you'll find it really difficult to overcome obstacles. Motivation simply isn't going to cut it because feeling motivated relies on dopamine, and as you know, most ADHD brains are dopamine-deficient.

Skill 5: Manage Your Mood Effectively

Changing your perspectives and learning to manage your outlook on life will positively affect your behaviors. As such, it's critical that you actively control your mood, choosing to regulate your emotions and see the positive in every situation you're facing.

Be careful with your words because what you say can also affect how well you're able to focus. The old adage by Henry Ford, "Whether you think you can, or you think you can't, you're right," is extremely pertinent to people with ADHD.

Skill 6: Build Healthy Habits

Your lifestyle will have a profound effect on your ability to achieve your goals and function in life. Ensuring that you are getting enough sleep, eating a varied and healthy diet, getting exercise, and spending time in nature are all necessary to help you manage stress and have a healthy body and mind.

Evaluating your processes and behaviors, instituting time management strategies, and ensuring you are effectively managing your stress will help you deal with the symptoms of ADHD and ensure you set yourself up for success.

Chapter 6

Boosting Your Emotional Quotient (EQ)

A lot of focus is placed on intellectual quotient (IQ) when kids are growing up. While some parents encourage emotional regulation, empathy, and emotional awareness, often these skills are overlooked.

For men with ADHD, emotional regulation can be one of the most disregarded facets of having the condition. Emotional outbursts and an inability to empathize fully with others are often labeled as symptoms of ADHD. When little boys grow into men, however, deficits in EQ can cause many problems, not just in personal relationships but in the workplace too.

Before getting into the reasons why EQ is important and the strategies available to help you develop your EQ, you need to understand the difference between IQ and EQ.

IQ Versus EQ

IQ (intellectual quotient) is a measurable and standardized score for

ascertaining a person's intelligence achieved via a test. An IQ test aims to accurately assess a person's cognitive capacity for reasoning and thinking. While it has been seen as controversial over the years, it is still a measure of intelligence for people across age groups.

EQ (emotional quotient), on the other hand, is a measure of how capable a person is of identifying their own emotions as well as those of others. Higher levels of EQ help people distinguish between their emotions, feelings, and moods and are used as a guide for social behaviors when interacting with other people.

The differences between EQ and IQ are as follows:

• The testing processes are both standardized, but each test requires participants to solve different questions about emotions and intelligence.

• EQ directly relates to a person's ability to succeed in life, whereas IQ relates to a person's ability to succeed academically.

• People are born with an IQ, whereas EQ is learned and acquired throughout life.

• People with an adequate EQ have great social relationships as they can express their emotions and perceive others'. A high IQ allows for a deeper understanding of data and information as well as its processing.

Emotional dysregulation occurs in people with ADHD because of executive dysfunction issues, stress, medication side effects, learned behaviors, and impulsiveness. When a person experiences emotional dysregulation, they have a hard time identifying and managing their own emotions and feelings, as well as ascertaining what other people are feeling.

Emotional outbursts, a perceived lack of empathy, and anxiety all affect a person's ability to form healthy, functioning social and personal relationships. This social exclusion and isolation can become problematic as a person often becomes depressed, which compounds their dysregulation as they don't have a chance to practice their EQ skills.

Why Emotional Regulation Is Needed for Well-Being

How we act when feeling our emotions is often the inner compass that guides us in our social interactions and building relationships. Not processing our emotions properly can cause all sorts of issues for us, not just because of our reactions but also because of how others perceive us as a result of them.

Added to this, we may act or interact incorrectly when trying to judge how others are feeling, or we simply cannot put ourselves in another person's position to empathize with them.

Emotional regulation occurs in three stages:

1. The initiating of emotions—an emotional trigger.

2. The inhibition of actions—acting, not reacting, to emotions.

3. The modulation of responses—understanding why there was an emotion.

With ADHD, steps two and three are often interrupted, and as such, an emotion is initiated with a resultant reaction occurring. In other words, we break the regulation chain, creating dysregulated emotions.

The reasons for this are not clear. They could relate to the way the ADHD brain processes stimuli or might be learned behavior. What is important to know is that emotional dysregulation occurs more often in ADHD men.

Emotional regulation acts as a modifier or buffer that helps us filter out what is essential to our safety and mental well-being and what is not. When we are dysregulated, we cannot discern what is safe, and as such, we live in a perpetual state of anxiety. When we become emotionally intelligent, we learn to regulate our emotions, lowering our anxiety and boosting our social relationships and feelings of belonging.

Other benefits of emotional regulation include:

• improved physical and mental well-being

• better performance at work

- better interpersonal and intrapersonal relationships

- greater self-awareness

Once you know the benefits of emotional regulation and can understand why being emotionally dysregulated affects your EQ, it becomes easy to assign a purpose to the strategies you will use to improve your emotional intelligence.

Strategies for Improving Emotional Intelligence

Before we dive into the strategies you can use to improve your emotional intelligence, let's take a look at the four attributes associated with EQ:

1. **The ability to self-manage:** When you are in control of your impulses, you're better able to manage your behaviors. Self-management is developed by finding healthy ways to control your emotions, take the initiative and responsibility for your actions, and follow through with what you have promised.

2. **The ability to be self-aware:** Being self-aware is the art of recognizing your emotions and how they may affect your behavior, thoughts, and interactions.

3. **The ability to be socially aware:** Empathy is the primary sign of social awareness, but other signs include being able to notice social cues, read the room, and be socially comfortable.

4. **The ability to manage relationships:** Finally, EQ is being able to maintain great relationships through proper conflict resolution, communication, and the ability to inspire others.

These attributes are directly linked to the four critical skills you require to develop to improve your EQ. These strategies are purely informational for now, but there are exercises in Chapter 7 that will assist in building upon your EQ.

Self-Management

To improve your EQ, you first need to be able to identify your emotions. Once you know what your emotions are, you can then make good decisions about what to do with them and how to resolve them constructively.

Often, stress overwhelms those of us with ADHD, and it can be very difficult to make a rational decision when we are stressed and emotional. You should acknowledge that while emotions are needed to keep us safe, a lot of the time, they're not rational or even factual.

Because of the stress we're carrying around with us, reacting to something based on perception can be very detrimental to personal relationships. Others may begin to view us as irrational or unpredictable.

Most of the time, our emotions have more to do with ourselves than other people. By learning to self-manage, we have the unique opportunity to work on our thoughts and behaviors rather than externalizing them and lashing out at others. Managing stress, therefore, is the primary focus and strategy required when learning self-management as a skill for EQ development.

Self-Awareness

Managing stress is a great way to begin self-managing. However, you will also need to be aware of your emotional experiences, your perception of life, what is triggering your emotions, and consistently be introspective so that you can deal with your thought patterns.

All of these qualities can be learned and are part of self-awareness. You must acknowledge that your emotions are not horrible experiences that happen to you. They are, in fact, valuable assets you can use in your life to develop yourself as well as your relationships.

Distancing yourself from your emotions is counterproductive, as is not taking responsibility for your actions when you don't manage your responses. However, if you aren't self-aware, understanding your emotions in a way that helps you respond appropriately can be difficult.

Social Awareness

Being socially aware is a key component to developing empathy, which is a fundamental aspect of EQ. You will need to learn to read cues in social settings so that you can assess the emotional state of others.

But social awareness goes beyond verbal communication; becoming aware of nonverbal cues is equally important. This requires concentration and a willingness to "read the room" before interrupting or sharing your point of view.

Relationship Management

The final piece to developing your EQ is to learn relationship management. Your relationships go beyond romantic ones and extend to your close friends and family too. People with ADHD can often have great social relationships and be the life of the party, but their close relationships suffer.

This is because we aren't comfortable showing acquaintances our true selves, but we are comfortable with our loved ones seeing the worst parts of us.

Part of relationship management is regulating our emotions so that we can communicate how we are feeling, but it is also the ability to see things from another person's perspective.

This is why relationship management is the final piece of the EQ puzzle. We have to self-manage, be self-aware, and develop empathy to have healthy close relationships.

Managing Stress

As you know, many men with ADHD live in a state of constant stress. Difficulty remaining focused, being surrounded by too many stimuli to process, being mindful of behaviors and moods, and the inability to remain still can all contribute to this stress and increase anxiety.

In addition, the desire to live up to others' expectations of us and feeling guilty when we don't succeed can just compound our stress. Managing our stress is a crucial facet of our life that will help us not only achieve our goals but also effectively regulate our emotions. However, for people with ADHD, normal techniques like meditation may not be enough.

Your first line of defense against stress should be to use tried-and-tested methods like:

• closing your eyes and focusing on your breath for a count of 20

• stretching for five minutes

• walking around for five minutes

If these techniques don't work, try the steps below on a daily basis to help effectively manage the stress caused by ADHD.

1. Don't Live In Denial

Blaming your behaviors on ADHD is not going to help you in the long run. You have to acknowledge your ADHD, get a proper diagnosis, keep up-to-date with your treatment plan, and work toward your goals.

2. Know Your Options

ADHD is no longer a one-treatment condition, and you have a world of treatment options available to you. For some people, medication is an absolute necessity, but for others, therapy, proper planning, and time management are enough to help you live a happy, functioning life.

3. Acknowledge that Time Isn't Fluid

Time may be fluid for you, but for other people, it is not. If you're working for someone who is flexible, you can negotiate and come to a compromise. If you're working for someone who is very rigid about timescales, explain that you sometimes have difficulty with them due to your ADHD. You could say you will implement your own reminder system but would appreciate their support (or another colleague's help) to keep you on track.

4. Set Clear Boundaries

There is absolutely no shame in having ADHD. Often, the best way to reduce your stress is to set boundaries and ask others to respect them. If you're easily distracted and working on developing your focus, speak to the people around you. Ask them to make sure they do not contribute to your distractions or request that others ensure you adhere to your reminders and alarms.

5. Embrace Structure and Routine

Structure and routine will be two of the most useful tools you develop as a man with ADHD. Make sure that you are reframing your point of view on structure and routine, moving away from the belief that they create a boring or mundane life. Routine is great—it stabilizes your body's rhythms, increases sleep quality, and reduces anxiety.

6. Set Aside Time for Fun

No one is saying you can't have fun and should just move from one routine or task to the next. It's important that you take time to do the things you love doing so that you can unwind and prevent yourself from burning out.

7. Remain Aware

It's easy to become comfortable or complacent when new routines are created and they work. Yet the nature of ADHD and the fact that most people have developed poor habits throughout their lives make it easy to slip back into old ways.

Learning to self-regulate and become emotionally intelligent are invaluable skills for anyone, but they are especially essential for men with ADHD. Our upbringing, societal constructs of how little boys are meant to act, and a brain that doesn't function neurotypically all contribute to lowered EQ. The brain, however, can change, and with training and awareness, EQ can be improved so that every ADHD man can reap the benefits of emotional intelligence.

Part Three

Improved Memory and Functioning

Chapter 7

The Power of Neuroplasticity

Our brain's ability to adapt, change, and develop is called neuroplasticity. In the past, it was thought that neuroplasticity stopped by the time we reached adolescence and that the brain had no more capacity to learn new skills.

It was later discovered that the brain's ability to adapt, change, reorganize information, and even grow new neural networks is a lifelong capability. This is good news for people with ADHD because it means you can choose to develop new skills to help you manage the symptoms of your condition.

Neuroplasticity is categorized into two parts:

1. **Functional plasticity:** The ability of the brain to move functions from damaged or underdeveloped areas to functioning areas.

2. **Structural plasticity:** The ability to change the physical structure of the brain as a result of learning new things.

The benefits of neuroplasticity include:

- learning new things and retaining this information

- improving and enhancing cognitive functions

- recovering from brain injuries

- strengthening areas that are not functioning correctly

- improving brain fitness

Once you know that neuroplasticity is beneficial to you and has the potential to improve the quality of your life, you can begin to set goals for yourself and your self-development.

A Word on Self-Love and Self-Growth

Men with ADHD can sometimes be hypercritical of themselves. We fight our bodies and our brains. This isn't fair because our brains work differently than neurotypical ones, and we have our own superpowers we could be tapping into. Yet we're too busy hating ourselves and listening to the inner critic in our minds.

All of this means that there are many of us walking around preconditioned to believe that self-growth and self-development are things that need to be done without self-love. We only believe that we are meant to be proud of ourselves when we get things right or when we're striving for the closest definition of perfection we can reach.

Human beings are not designed to be perfect. In fact, it is in our very design to be imperfect because it is only through our mistakes that we ever learn, develop, and grow. Before you do the exercises below to learn to manage your symptoms and develop your mind, I want you to know that you *should* love yourself exactly where you are.

It's perfectly acceptable to celebrate your successes and also to honor how far you've traveled and how much adversity you've overcome. Being loved and loving yourself is a powerful motivator. Plus, when you love yourself, you're far more likely to want to become the best person you can be.

The exercises below are based on cognitive behavioral therapy (CBT) and dialectical behavior therapy (DBT) techniques, which are incredibly effective in the management of the symptoms of ADHD.

Exercise 1: Improve Working Memory

This exercise is designed to train your brain in word retrieval as well as develop critical thinking and neural agility. Fill in the form below and practice this exercise daily. Remember to add new words in the blank columns below so that your brain is challenged every time you do the exercise.

Question	Answer	Spell Both Words Backward
What rhymes with cat?		
What rhymes with jar?		
What rhymes with hair?		
What rhymes with gate?		
What rhymes with mouse?		
What is the opposite of fast?		
What is the opposite of short?		
What is the opposite of hot?		
What is the opposite of up?		

Question	Answer	Spell the Answer Backward
Name a color	115	
Name a sport		
Name a vegetable		
Name a wild animal		
What is the 7th month of the year?		
What is the 4th month of the year?		
What is the 10th month of the year?		
What is your name?		
What is the name of one of your pets?		

Exercise 2: ADHD Brain Training

This activity is designed not only to train your brain, but also to assist you in learning how to control your frustration and push through obstacles and challenging situations. Trust me when I say this exercise can be extremely frustrating!

Completing this exercise will help your mind begin to focus on smaller details, honing in on what you're asking it to focus on rather than the bigger picture. Try to persevere, and over time, your brain will begin to find new ways to complete the tasks assigned to it.

Instructions

- Get two pieces of blank paper.

- Place one sheet of paper on your right and the other on your left.

- Get two pencils, placing one in each hand.

- Now, simultaneously draw a vertical line on each piece of paper using both your left and right hands.

- Repeat this three times.

- Next, draw a triangle with both hands. If this is too easy for you, draw a triangle with one hand and a square with the other.

- Now, draw a circle with both hands. If this is too easy for you, draw a circle with one hand and a triangle with the other.

- Next, draw a square with both hands. If this is too easy for you, draw a circle with your other hand.

- Are you still with me? Things are about to get a little more challenging...

- Draw a circle on one page, a square on the other page, and lift your foot off the floor at the same time.

- Now switch the pattern assigned to each hand and your foot.

If you find yourself becoming overly frustrated, slow it down, find the humor in the exercise, and remind yourself that even neurotypicals find this exercise to be extremely challenging.

Exercise 3: Improving Focus and Concentration

This exercise is designed to help you focus and concentrate, even with visual stimulation present. Try to complete one line every day of the week, and then use Google to find similar worksheets.

The first column is the letter or number you need to find. Subsequent columns will contain visually similar numbers or letters that you will need to filter out.

A	d	d	d	d	d	a	d	d	d	d	d	d	d	d	a	d	a	d	d	d	d	d	d
d	b	b	b	b	b	b	b	b	b	b	d	b	b	b	b	b	b	d	b	b	b	b	b
6	9	9	9	9	9	9	9	9	9	6	9	9	9	9	9	9	9	9	9	6	9	9	9
9	6	6	6	6	6	6	6	9	6	6	6	6	6	6	6	6	6	9	6	9	6	6	6
p	q	q	q	q	q	q	p	q	q	q	q	q	q	q	q	q	q	q	p	q	q	q	q
3	8	8	8	8	8	8	8	8	8	8	8	3	8	8	8	8	8	8	8	8	3	8	8
I	i	i	i	i	i	i	i	i	i	I	i	i	i	I	i	I	i	i	i	i	i	i	i

Exercise 4: Building Empathy

This worksheet is designed to help you see things from another person's perspective. Once you can begin to empathize with others, it is easier to look at your own behaviors and words and how they are affecting other people.

When someone has confronted you about your behavior, completing this worksheet before you react is an amazing way to build emotional intelligence and a great relationship.

A note on this exercise: Please remember that becoming empathetic does not mean agreeing with everyone or accepting behaviors that are toxic for you. It simply means understanding that people see the world differently from you and then deciding what the appropriate response is for you.

Instructions

• Get your journal or a piece of paper and a pen or pencil.

• Try to calm your mind and ground yourself in the present by focusing on your breath.

• When you are ready, recall a situation that caused conflict or in which you were unable to understand a person's reaction to your behavior.

• Write this situation down at the top of your page.

• Now, take a moment to think about what you were thinking just before you acted.

• Write your thoughts down.

• Next, take a moment to think about how you felt at that moment.

• Write this down.

• Think about how you acted or reacted at that moment.

• Write this down.

• Finally, think about the consequences of your actions at that moment.

• If you begin to feel irritated, frustrated, or emotional at any point, stop and return your focus to your breath.

• Once you are calm, repeat the steps above, but replace your thoughts, feelings, and actions with those of the other person.

Here is an example:

I interrupted a friend while they were talking about something important to them. I thought they had been talking for a while. I felt that the conversation was boring and wanted to speak about something more interesting to me. I acted by stepping into the conversation and speaking over my friend. The consequence of my actions was that my friend got upset and walked away from the conversation.

Reverse this so that you can see it from the other person's perspective.

My friend interrupted me while I was talking about something important to me. I thought it was disrespectful. I felt disrespected at that moment and became angry and hurt. I stepped away from the conversation because I didn't want to lash out, hurt my friend's feelings, or embarrass anyone.

In reversing the situation, it is apparent that the behavior caused the other person emotional pain. Even if you don't understand why it caused them pain, you can understand their reaction better because you know what emotional pain feels like.

Exercise 5: Managing Anxiety—RAIN

Mindfulness is the state of being able to observe our thoughts without judgment or rationality, creating a sense of awareness about how we feel without an emotional response occurring.

As you know from reading the previous chapters, being mindful is really important when dealing with and managing anxiety effectively. RAIN is a mindfulness practice that helps your mind stay grounded in the present, especially when you're experiencing thoughts and emotions that may be uncomfortable.

It stands for recognize, allow, investigate, and nurture.

Using the table below, fill in your anxious thought spiral in the RAIN section in exercise 8 and follow the instructions.

Recognize	Seek to uncover the thought you're having that is causing you anxiety. Recognize this thought consciously, as well as the feelings you're having. Name your feelings out loud or say them silently to yourself.
Allow	Observe yourself as if you were outside of your body. Imagine yourself as an actor, and you're watching yourself play out a scene. Let go of your judgments and allow yourself to feel whatever it is you're feeling.
Investigate	Notice your thoughts in detail. What words are being used? Where do you believe your thoughts and feelings are coming from? Take a moment to reflect on what you need in this moment.
Nurture	Begin to comfort yourself, expressing words of acceptance, self-love, and gratitude. Let yourself know that you're okay, that you are loved, and that emotions only last 90 seconds. Take deep breaths, letting healing, cleansing air into your body, and exhaling your anxiety.

Exercise 6: Self-Regulation Exercise—Mindfulness Meditation

Because the ADHD brain is often overstimulated, it can become easy to feel overwhelmed by the emotional responses to external and internal stimuli. Mindfulness meditation, as you know, is a fantastic way to quiet and calm the ADHD mind before reacting to our emotions and is a cornerstone of self-regulation.

In the beginning stages of learning how to practice mindfulness meditation, you may want to allocate a specifically dedicated space that you keep clean and free of clutter. If you live with other people, you should ask them not to disturb you during your meditation time.

1. Sit in a comfortable, quiet space. Straighten your back and face forward. Make sure that you're not too relaxed in your seating posture; you don't want to fall asleep!

If sitting on the floor is not for you, you can sit in a comfortable, upright chair that supports your back. Make sure your feet can touch the ground, and place the soles of your feet flat on the floor.

Place the palms of your hands flat on your thighs and close your eyes if you would like to.

Now, take a deep breath in through your nose. Inhale for a count of four, and exhale through your mouth for a count of four.

<u>Repeat these circular cleansing breaths five times.</u>

2. As I mentioned before, you do not have to clear your mind. In fact, it's very normal for your thoughts to wander, especially when you're trying not to think of anything.

Instead of frustrating yourself trying to clear your mind, observe your thoughts and allow them to pass naturally.

If you find yourself fixating or ruminating on one thought, acknowledge it without judgment and then return your attention to your breath.

Consciously take a moment to inhale for a count of four through your nose and exhale for a count of four through your mouth, repeating this process five times.

If the thought persists, choose to replace it with a mantra or saying.

Keep it simple, instructing your body to "breathe in and breathe out," or simply ask yourself to be calm while focusing on your breath.

3. Finally, be kind to yourself.

The reality is that you have ADHD and have spent your whole life giving in to your urges or trying to release your energy by fidgeting and moving.

If you find that the urge to scratch, fidget, or twitch is overwhelming, allow yourself to do it and then return to your practice.

Over time, these urges will diminish, and you will begin to notice that the time between them begins to lengthen.

When starting your mindfulness meditation practices, try to aim for five minutes of remaining seated and focusing on your breath. Once you have built a tolerance for these five minutes, add another session to your day, instead of extending your time in meditation. Your goal should be to have three five-minute mindfulness meditation slots during your day.

Exercise 7: Time Management Exercise—Time Blocking

The worksheet below is designed to help you effectively time-block your day so you are not overwhelmed by your tasks. This can be used in conjunction with a calendar that will remind you to shift slots or blocks.

Feel free to label blocks 1 through 4, anything you like. For example, block 1 could be the morning routine; block 2 could be prioritized work tasks; block 3 could be non-priority work tasks and home-priority tasks, and so on.

The blocks that should *not* be changed are the goal for the day and the sleep routine blocks.

Day: Monday	
My goal today is: Arrive at work on time	
Block 1	7:00 – Wake up and walk the dog
	7:30 – Have breakfast and make lunch
	8:00 – Drive to work
	9:00 – Arrive at office and attend morning briefing
	9:30 – Check and respond to emails
	BREAK
Block 2	11:00 – Finance meeting
	12:00 –Lunch
	13:00-15:30 – Regional meeting
	BREAK
Block 3	16:00 – Go to the grocery store
	16:30 - Drive home
	17:30 – Prepare and have dinner
	BREAK
Block 4	19:00 – Family time
	20:00 – Go for a walk
	21:00 – Read a book

Sleep Routine	22:00 – 23:00
	
	   • Hygiene ritual
	   • Meditation
	   • Stretching exercises
	   • Set the sleep environment

Day:	
My goal today is:	
Block 1	
	BREAK
Block 2	
	BREAK
Block 3	
	BREAK
Block 4	
Sleep Routine	Start time: • • • •

Exercise 8: Calm the Overthinking Brain by Decluttering

Brain decluttering can also be called brain dumping, and it is an effective way to clear your mind of all of the thoughts you have surrounding your pending tasks for the day ahead.

Here is an example of what a completed brain dump looks like. A blank version, plus more instructions, are below this table so you can copy it and do this process regularly.

Work through one category at a time.

Brain Dump Worksheet

Category 1: Home	**Category 2: Work**
- Do the laundry more often	- Prioritize my workload
- Set up direct debits for paying bills	- Arrive on time every day
- I feel overwhelmed by everything after working all day	- Confide in someone about my ADHD –hopefully, it will help
- Get the kids to do some chores	- I feel like I look disorganized most of the time
Category 3: Family/Kids	**Category 4: Me**
- Spend more quality time with the kids	- I need to find other ways to relax and switch off my mind
- Lose my patience less with my partner	- Get back into hobbies I had when I was younger
- Worried things are getting too much and it will affect my family	- Connect more with old friends
- Visit my parents more	- Talk more about what's going on with me

Brain Dump Worksheet

Using the table provided below, write down all of your thoughts and pending tasks pertaining to the areas of your life.

Complete one category at a time.

Category 1: Home	**Category 2: Work**
Category 3: Family/Kids	**Category 4: Me**

Your brain dump information will then be used to complete the following exercise.

Exercise 9: Priority List

Once you have written down all of your thoughts and tasks for one specific category, highlight or circle any important tasks and move them to the first block in the priority list below. Any remaining tasks should go in the "Non-priority tasks" section. Now write the priority tasks that you want to focus on in the "Activities to be added to the time blocking sheet." Any negative or critical thoughts should be written in the final block, so that you can use the RAIN exercise to investigate and deal with the feelings and thoughts you're having.

Other thoughts can be discarded or ignored. A great way to deal with all of the clutter in your mind once you have written it out on this worksheet is to tear up the exercise page and take five minutes for mindfulness meditation.

Priority tasks	1 2 3 4 5 6
Non-Priority tasks	1 2 3 4 5 6
Activities to be added to the time blocking sheet:	1 2 3 4 5 6
Write down any negative or critical thoughts here to use the RAIN exercise with.	1 2 3 4 5 6

As previously mentioned, these exercises are based on (CBT) and (DBT) which are proven techniques to manage ADHD symptoms. Take the time to incorporate one exercise at a time in your daily routine. You may want to start with the easiest one. When you master it, you can move to the next exercise, and so on. Once you get into the habit of doing these exercises daily, it will help you manage your ADHD positively so that you can begin to thrive.

Chapter 8

Thriving With ADHD

ADHD is a lifelong condition with no cure. This doesn't mean you need to suffer with your symptoms, though. With therapy, self-care, medication, and a willingness to work on your behaviors, you can begin to thrive with ADHD.

Remember, ADHD comes with its own set of superpowers, but it's up to you to unlock them by using the resources available to you. This last chapter is dedicated to the self-care and lifestyle changes you can make to help enhance your superpowers to become the best man you can possibly be.

Before you read the information below, I'd like you to take a moment to remind yourself that your definition of success is yours alone. You don't need to be anyone else, nor do you have to build a life that isn't uniquely yours.

Why Self-Care Is Important

Self-care is extremely important for men with ADHD to help reduce the symptoms of the condition and bring focus to taking care of our bodies and minds. Concentrating on our symptoms and having to deal with an enormous amount of stimuli daily can be mentally and physically exhausting. When we neglect our bodies, it can become even harder to focus on everyday tasks. Prioritizing self-care is a form of self-love that will greatly improve our quality of life and is one of the critical steps in achieving success when it comes to our goals for ourselves.

Many men think that self-care is something only women do, and when asked, they usually define it as trips to the spa, massages, pedicures, and so on. Now, there is absolutely nothing wrong with men participating in these activities. In fact, I encourage you to try at least one of these every month. But they are an added bonus on top of a great self-care routine.

Self-care includes:

• creating a great sleep routine for good sleep

• getting enough exercise

• eating nutritious, healthy meals

• reducing clutter in your home and mind

• creating a daily schedule that is routine

• practicing exercises for improved concentration, emotional regulation, and organization

In addition to the list above, self-care is the prioritization of your needs so that you can build self-love and self-esteem.

Healthy Lifestyle Habits for Men With ADHD

Now that you know why self-care is important, let's break down each area so it's easier for you to incorporate them into your life.

Sleep and Sleep Routines

Getting enough quality sleep is essential for the health of your brain and body. For people with ADHD, sleep is often viewed as a waste of time, but proper, restorative sleep helps with mood regulation, attention span, and memory, as well as the healing of the body.

Creating a sleep routine that facilitates proper restorative sleep can be challenging for men with ADHD, as poor habits may have led to circadian rhythm issues. The great news is that with a little persistence, you can reclaim your sleep and reap the benefits of proper rest.

Here are a few tips:

1. Move away from technology and screens an hour before your bedtime. If you haven't set a time to get into bed, do it now.

2. Make sure you're free of distractions an hour before you go to sleep. These distractions can include scrolling through social media, gaming, or starting the next episode of your favorite show. Instead, choose to do the quick chores that need to be done in your home, like packing the dishwasher or doing a brief tidy-up. That way, you can wake up to a clean, orderly home the next day, ensuring you can stay on track with your schedule. Set a timer for 30 minutes for these tasks and assign them to the first half of your sleep routine.

3. The last 30 minutes of your sleep routine should include personal hygiene, including a warm bath or shower, brushing your teeth, reading, and meditating.

4. Set a reminder to get into bed and stick to it. Even if you lie in the dark for a while, that's fine. The point is to allow your mind and body to begin training themselves to go to sleep earlier.

If you've been practicing great sleep hygiene for more than a month and your mind is still resisting sleep, you may want to consider a melatonin supplement. Always consult with your healthcare professional before taking new medications. Make sure you read the instructions for your melatonin, take it a few hours before you sleep, and understand that long-term melatonin use can hinder sleep routines.

Exercise for Men With ADHD

Getting sufficient exercise is beneficial for everyone, but for the ADHD man, it allows for the release of pent-up energy and provides an external outlet for internalized hyperactivity symptoms.

For men with ADHD, it's important to find interesting, engaging, and exciting exercise options that will keep them from getting bored. When coupled with great nutrition, exercise is one of the most powerful tools for helping to release energy, regulate mood, and deal with stress and anxiety.

1. Set realistic exercise goals for yourself, especially if you are currently sedentary. Aim for 15 minutes of vigorous exercise every second day to begin with, working your way up to a maximum of one hour every day of the week. Change your routines and incorporate different types of exercise so that you remain interested.

2. Make sure your exercise is moderate to vigorous. You should be breathing hard but not exhausted.

3. Do activities that involve different muscle groups and build upon motor skills at least twice a week. These can include martial arts, dancing, or ball sports.

Make sure to nourish your body properly both before and after working out, and look for natural forms of protein and amino acids rather than consuming convenient shakes or protein bars. These convenience products often contain ingredients that exacerbate hyperactive symptoms.

Nutrition for Men With ADHD

The ADHD brain requires certain vitamins and minerals in higher quantities. As the brain is made up mostly of fat, which is responsible for neural brain signaling, an increase in omega-3 fatty acids is essential for the ADHD brain.

Nutrients like zinc, iron, and vitamin D are also essential for proper brain signaling, and these nutrients are often lacking in modern convenience foods. One of the biggest challenges men with ADHD face is the inability to complete multi-step tasks, making cooking a real chore. It is, however, essential to learn how to cook properly so that you can nourish your body. Once you find the excitement and creativity in cooking, it can be a lot of fun.

1. Start small when making dietary changes. Getting rid of everything unhealthy all at once can feel overwhelming or like a punishment.

2. Significantly reduce stimulant foods like coffee, tea, and energy drinks. Eliminating these is actually best, but a reduction can also make a difference.

3. Make sure you're getting enough zinc, iron, and vitamin D from natural sources like fatty fish, avocados, leafy greens, and eggs.

4. Become mindful of and eliminate foods that trigger symptoms or make them worse.

Everyone's body is different regarding nutrition, but general eating guidelines are to make sure you're consuming larger meals in the middle of the day, fueling your body properly before and after exercise, and eating mineral- and nutrition-rich foods.

Healthy Support Systems

Building a healthy support system is important as it can help you through tough times, be there when you want to bounce ideas off someone, provide positive feedback, and celebrate your victories.

Structured support systems are often in the form of support groups that are geared toward helping people with ADHD and may include professionals who offer guidance and resources. Informal support systems usually include friends and family who understand or empathize with your struggles and provide emotional and physical aid.

Having both of these support systems in your life will help you get the most out of building a positive group of people. They will assist you in reaching your goals and in dealing with the specific challenges you face.

With these people around you, you can gain valuable insights and empower yourself in how to manage your symptoms properly. All of this, of course, means being able to thrive in your life.

The aims of joining support groups and creating a network of positively influential people in your life are:

• encouraging and maintaining new behaviors

• reinforcing good behaviors

• bringing attention to symptoms that need to be managed

• sharing knowledge and experiences

• offering emotional support

• learning empathy for other people's struggles

Success is a lonely journey if you do not have anyone to share it with. Having people in your life who can love and support you will provide you with more motivation to succeed.

Conclusion

Thriving isn't about making life comfortable, fun, and happy; it's about finding purpose and making our own unique contribution.

Malcolm Stern

ADHD may come with a high level of stigma attached to it, and for the men who live with it, this stigma can often cause a lot of anxiety, guilt, and shame. Getting a diagnosis doesn't need to be this way, though, and finding out why life feels challenging at times is the first step in learning the tools required to unlock your ADHD superpowers.

Practicing the tools provided helps us to manage our symptoms and stick to the treatment plans. Ultimately, this will enhance our quality of life and improve everything from our ability to be productive to emotional regulation and even our relationships.

If you have just received an ADHD diagnosis, it's okay and natural to feel overwhelmed. If you've been aware of your ADHD for a while but haven't quite known where to start when it comes to at-home tools, you've taken the right steps toward your symptom management future.

Using the exercises and information available in this book, like mind mapping, time-blocking, mindfulness meditation, executive functioning, improving your EQ, etc., are great add-ons to your conventional therapy and other prescribed treatments.

Before finishing this book and putting the information and exercises into practice, I want you to know that you're not alone. There are so many men out there, some that you know of and most that you don't, who took steps to manage their ADHD. It was through this management that they found their definition of success in the same way that you can.

Olympic champion Michael Phelps was nine when he was diagnosed with severe ADHD. With his mother's guidance, Phelps used his interest in swimming to help him focus on his schoolwork, ultimately leading to successfully weaning himself off medication. Today, Phelps has 22 Olympic medals—the most any athlete has ever won.

Grammy-award singer Justin Timberlake has been public about his ADHD and OCD struggles, but also credits his success to the tools he was taught to manage his symptoms. Also, comedian and presenter Howie Mandel, with the support of his wife and parents, has overcome ADHD, becoming the spokesperson for the 'Adult ADHD is Real' campaign.

Even billionaire Bill Gates, the founder of Microsoft, has tapped into his ADHD superpowers to become one of the richest men in the world, using a lot of his wealth as a contributor to charities.

You see, living with ADHD doesn't mean you need to struggle through life. In fact, when you unlock your ADHD superpowers, learn to love yourself, and embrace your self-growth journey to gain deeper insight into just how wonderfully unique you are, ADHD has the potential to be the very source of your quest for a thriving life.

You now have the tools and information you need to live a life that is successful, loving, and as amazingly unique as you are. I would love to hear about your journey with ADHD and how this book has helped you, so please feel free to leave a review and a comment so that others know they're not alone.

References

Alder, S. (n.d.). *Adhd Quotes*. Goodreads. https://www.goodreads.com/quotes/tag/adhd

Alhawatmeh, H. N., Rababa, M., Alfaqih, M., Albataineh, R., Hweidi, I., & Abu Awwad, A. (2022). The Benefits of Mindfulness Meditation on Trait Mindfulness, Perceived Stress, Cortisol, and C-Reactive Protein in Nursing Students: A Randomized Controlled Trial. *Advances in Medical Education and Practice, Volume 13*, 47–58. https://doi.org/10.2147/amep.s348062

Amen, D. G. (2001). *Healing ADD*. Penguin.

Asarnow, R. F., Newman, N., Weiss, R. E., & Su, E. (2021). Association of Attention-Deficit/Hyperactivity Disorder Diagnoses With Pediatric Traumatic Brain Injury. *JAMA Pediatrics*. https://doi.org/10.1001/jamapediatrics.2021.2033

Balogh, L., Pulay, A. J., & Réthelyi, J. M. (n.d.). *Genetics in the ADHD Clinic: How Can Genetic Testing Support the Current Clinical Practice?* Frontiersin. https://www.frontiersin.org/articles/10.3389/fpsyg.2022.751041/full

Beheshti, A., Chavanon, M.-L., & Christiansen, H. (2020). Emotion dysregulation in adults with attention deficit hyperactivity disorder: a meta-analysis. *BMC Psychiatry, 20*. https://doi.org/10.1186/s12888-020-2442-7

Belmont, J. (2017) *CBT Technique: Using the Triple Column Technique to Change Your Thoughts to Change Your Life!* PsychCentral. https://psychcentral.com/pro/psychoeducation/2017/07/cbt-technique-using-the-triple-column-technique-to-change-your-thoughts-to-change-your-life#1

Carnegie, A. (n.d). Goodreads. https://www.goodreads.com/quotes/122624-if-you-want-to-be-happy-set-a-goal-that

Champ, R. E., Adamou, M., & Tolchard, B. (2021). The impact of psychological theory on the treatment of Attention Deficit Hyperactivity Disorder (ADHD) in adults: A scoping review. *PLOS ONE, 16*(12), e0261247. https://doi.org/10.1371/journal.pone.0261247

Covey, S. (n.d.). *Stephen R. Covey Quotes*. Goodreads. https://bestbookbits.com/the-7-habits-of-highly-effective-people-powerful-lessons-in-personal-change-by-stephen-covey/

Donzelli, G., Carducci, A., Llopis-Gonzalez, A., Verani, M., Llopis-Morales, A., Cioni, L., & Morales-Suárez-Varela, M. (2019). The Association between Lead and Attention-Deficit/Hyperactivity Disorder: A Systematic Review. International *Journal of Environmental Research and Public Health, 16*(3), 382. https://doi.org/10.3390/ijerph16030382

Eddings, M. (n.d.). *Adhd Quotes*. Goodreads. https://www.goodreads.com/quotes/tag/adhd

Ford, H (n.d.). *Henry Ford Quotes*. Goodreads. https://www.goodreads.com/author/quotes/203714.Henry_Ford

Ghaemi, S. N. (2018). After the failure of DSM: clinical research on psychiatric diagnosis. *World Psychiatry, 17*(3), 301–302. https://doi.org/10.1002/wps.20563

Jensen, E. (n.d.). *Emotional Intelligence Quotes*. Sources of Insight. https://sourcesofinsight.com/emotional-intelligence-quotes/

References

Attention-deficit/hyperactivity disorder (ADHD) in children - Symptoms and causes. (2019, June 25). Mayo Clinic. https://www.mayoclinic.org/diseases-conditions/adhd/symptoms-causes/syc-20350889

Mercedes, S. (n.d.). *Adhd Quotes.* Goodreads. https://www.goodreads.com/quotes/tag/adhd

Millman, D. (n.d.). *Dan Millman Quotes.* Goodreads. https://www.goodreads.com/quotes/10158365-you-don-t-have-to-control-your-thoughts-you-just-have

Marti, M. (n.d.). *Thriving Quotes.* Goodreads. https://www.goodreads.com/quotes/tag/thriving

Montagna, A., Karolis, V., Batalle, D., Counsell, S., Rutherford, M., Arulkumaran, S., Happe, F., Edwards, D., & Nosarti, C. (2020). ADHD symptoms and their neurodevelopmental correlates in children born very preterm. *PLOS ONE, 15*(3), e0224343. https://doi.org/10.1371/journal.pone.0224343

Attention-Deficit/Hyperactivity Disorder (ADHD). (2014). National Institute of Mental Health. https://www.nimh.nih.gov/health/statistics/attention-deficit-hyperactivity-disorder-adhd

Pera, G. (2022, March 12). *Sleep Deprivation: ADHD Symptoms Keeping You Awake?* Additude Magazine. https://www.additudemag.com/wired-tired-sleep-deprived/

Rai, D. (n.d.). *Dharmendra Raj Quotes.* Goodreads. https://www.goodreads.com/quotes/11137481-it-is-not-easy-to-make-things-simple---one

Roth, R. M., & Saykin, A. J. (2004). Executive dysfunction in attention-deficit/hyperactivity disorder: cognitive and neuroimaging findings. *Psychiatric Clinics of North America, 27*(1), 83–96. https://doi.org/10.1016/s0193-953x(03)00112-6

Ryu, S., Choi, Y.-J., An, H., Kwon, H.-J., Ha, M., Hong, Y.-C., Hong, S.-J., & Hwang, H.-J. (2022). Associations between Dietary Intake and Attention Deficit Hyperactivity Disorder (ADHD) Scores by Repeated Measurements in School-Age Children. *Nutrients, 14*(14), 2919. https://doi.org/10.3390/nu14142919

Sarkis, S. (2011, July 21). Do People With ADHD Cheat More? *Psychology Today.*https://www.psychologytoday.com/intl/blog/here-there-and-everywhere/201107/do-people-adhd-cheat-more

Shapiro, S. (2016, January 20). Adult ADHD and Work: Improving Executive Function: 5 strategies to improve work performance. https://www.psychologytoday.com/us/blog/the-best-strategies-for-managing-adult-adhd/201601/adult-adhd-and-work-improving-executive?amp

Silver, Dr. L. (2023, March 28). *ADHD Symptoms Or ADHD Comorbidity? Diagnosing Related Conditions.* Additude Magazine. https://www.additudemag.com/when-its-not-just-adhd/#:~:text=At%20least%20half%20of%20all

Song, P., Zha, M., Yang, Q., Zhang, Y., Li, X., & Rudan, I. (2021). The prevalence of adult attention-deficit hyperactivity disorder: A global systematic review and meta-analysis. *Journal of Global Health, 11*(04009). https://doi.org/10.7189/jogh.11.04009

Spurgeon, C. (n.d.). *Charles Spurgeon Quotes.* Brainy Quote. https://www.brainyquote.com/quotes/charles_spurgeon_132220

Stern, M. (n.d.). *Malcolm Stern Quotes.* Goodreads. https://www.goodreads.com/quotes/10335289-thriving-isn-t-about-making-life-comfortable-fun-and-happy-it-s

Stevens, T. (2006). There Is No Meaningful Relationship Between Television Exposure and

References

Symptoms of Attention-Deficit/Hyperactivity Disorder. *PEDIATRICS, 117*(3), 665–672. https://doi.org/10.1542/peds.2005-0863

Weissenberger, S., Schonova, K., Büttiker, P., Fazio, R., Vnukova, M., Stefano, G. B., & Ptacek, R. (2021). Time Perception is a Focal Symptom of Attention-Deficit/Hyperactivity Disorder in Adults. *Medical Science Monitor, 27.* https://doi.org/10.12659/msm.933766

Wilens, T. E., & Spencer, T. J. (2010). Understanding Attention-Deficit/Hyperactivity Disorder from Childhood to Adulthood. *Postgraduate Medicine, 122*(5), 97–109. https://doi.org/10.3810/pgm.2010.09.2206

Men with Adult ADHD Workbook

80+ Proven Mind Mapping Exercises to Improve Time Management, Productivity, Creativity, and Executive Functioning by Eliminating Overthinking and Procrastination

Book 2

Introduction

Contrary to common misconceptions, ADHD is not limited to childhood. In fact, approximately 1 in 20 adult males, or 5.4%, live with this neurodevelopmental condition (Klein, 2021). While diagnostic rates are higher among men compared to women, the challenges posed by ADHD in adulthood for both sexes are significant and far-reaching, often impacting careers, personal relationships, and mental health in general.

The experience of ADHD can manifest differently in men compared to women, often influenced by societal expectations and perceptions. Men are more frequently diagnosed with ADHD, as the external symptoms they exhibit, like hyperactivity and impulsivity, tend to be more visible and disruptive. In contrast, women with ADHD often display inattentive symptoms. This disparity in symptom presentation can lead to a higher likelihood of diagnosis for men, as their behaviors are recognized as atypical faster.

While the manifestation of ADHD symptoms can vary among individuals, common indicators in adult men often fall into two main categories: inattention and hyperactivity-impulsivity. Inattentive symptoms may include difficulties sustaining focus, disorganization, forgetfulness, and avoidance of tasks requiring sustained mental effort. Hyperactive and impulsive behaviors can manifest as restlessness, excessive talking, fidgeting, and interrupting others.

It's important to note that the severity of these symptoms can also differ based on the specific ADHD subtype. These subtypes could be predominantly inattentive, predominantly hyperactive-impulsive, or a combination of both. While ADHD is a neurodevelopmental condition with roots in childhood, its impact on adult life can be profound and multifaceted, often in ways that may not be initially recognized or attributed to ADHD.

Moreover, while the outward manifestations of ADHD in men are more apparent, it's essential to recognize the internal experiences that may be less visible. Men with ADHD can also struggle with emotional dysregulation, risk-taking behaviors, and challenges in maintaining focus and organization.

Interestingly, some research suggests that ADHD symptoms, particularly hyperactivity, may be more likely to persist into adulthood for women than men. This could be attributed to the tendency for hyperactive behaviors to diminish with age, while inattentive symptoms often persist (Stibbe et al., 2020).

Regardless of gender, individuals with ADHD face an increased risk of comorbid conditions. More specifically, men with ADHD may be more prone to *externalized* challenges that include risk-taking behaviors such as substance abuse or impulsive behaviors.

In addition, men with ADHD often grapple with low self-esteem and a sense of hopelessness, underscoring the emotional and psychological impacts of this neurodevelopmental condition.

Nevertheless, it's crucial to recognize that an ADHD diagnosis does not define your inherent strengths, intelligence, or capabilities. With the right support strategies and management approaches, countless men with ADHD have not only learned to control their symptoms but also thrived in all aspects of their lives. For many, gaining insight into their diagnosis was the pivotal moment that catalyzed profound personal growth and positive transformation.

Regardless of your specific experiences or challenges, know that you possess the innate resilience and capability to thrive with ADHD. In reading *Men with Adult ADHD Workbook: 80+ Proven Mind Mapping Exercises to Improve Time Management, Productivity, Creativity, and Executive Functioning by Eliminating Overthinking and Procrastination,* you will discover how mind mapping can revolutionize your approach to managing the unique symptoms of ADHD as a man.

The truth is that ADHD does not diminish your worth or potential. Embracing evidence-based treatments and therapeutic interventions, like mind mapping, *can* empower you to cultivate the necessary skills to unlock your true potential.

Some of the methods or techniques mentioned in the exercises might not be familiar to you. To help with this, there is a Glossary at the end of the book. When a term is explained in the Glossary, it will be made clear.

Finally, you must know that ADHD is a real condition: it affects the brain's structure, chemistry, and function. However, the remarkable thing about the human brain is that it is *plastic* and can be rewired, rebalanced, and reshaped through repetitive actions. There is no shame in needing support, and the strength and courage you have shown in purchasing this book shows you're ready to make a change. ADHD is not a character flaw but a condition that can be overcome and managed with the tools you're about to use.

Chapter 1

Mind Mapping and Its Applications

Mind mapping is a revolutionary technique that allows us to organize our thoughts and ideas visually into connected groups. When using a mind map, we start with a central concept or subject and create a web, branching out into related subtopics, ideas, and themes to visualize our thoughts, emotions, and subconscious patterns.

While simple at first glance, mind mapping is a dynamic approach that mirrors how the human brain actually processes information—through associations, connections, and radiating thought patterns. By externalizing our cognitive processes onto a mind map, we can harness the full potential of our brain's natural way of thinking.

Although mind mapping can undoubtedly be used in every aspect of our lives, it is most often utilized to enhance productivity and focus, generate ideas, retain memory, manage time, and uncover the thoughts and beliefs that affect our well-being.

The Science Behind Mind Mapping

Mind mapping's effectiveness lies in engaging and integrating various cognitive processes within the brain. This powerful technique taps into our inherent capacity for associative thinking, allowing us to harness the very ways our minds naturally operate.

When mind mapping, we activate our brain's logical, analytical left hemisphere and the creative, intuitive right hemisphere. The structured, hierarchical organization and use of keywords stimulate left-brain processes like logic, sequence, and language. Simultaneously, the colors, images, and free-flowing associations spark right-brain activities centered on imagination, spatial awareness, and pattern recognition. Integrating these complementary modes of thinking creates a synergistic cognitive state that enhances our ability to process, retain, and generate information more effectively.

Research has consistently demonstrated the benefits of mind mapping across various domains, including learning, memory, creativity, and executive functioning—areas that ADHD often impacts. In a study published in the *Journal of Educational Psychology*, researchers found that people with ADHD who used mind mapping as a learning strategy exhibited significantly better comprehension and long-term retention of complex information than those who used more traditional note-taking methods (Kajka & Kulik, 2021).

Another study showed that mind mapping can boost creative thinking and idea generation. ADHD participants who engaged in mind mapping exercises demonstrated improved fluency, flexibility, and originality in their creative problem-solving abilities (Mareva et al., 2023).

Furthermore, mind mapping has shown promise in enhancing executive functioning skills, which are often compromised in people with ADHD. A study published in the *Journal of Attention Disorders* found that adults with ADHD who received mind mapping training experienced improvements in areas such as planning, organization, and cognitive flexibility (Sedgwick-Müller et al., 2022).

These are only a few of the significant scientific findings that show just how profound an impact mind mapping can have on cognitive processes. This makes it a powerful tool for those of us who want to optimize our brain's potential and mitigate the challenges associated with ADHD.

Mind Mapping for ADHD Management

For men with ADHD, mind mapping can be particularly helpful, not only in common areas like task organization and time management. It can also be valuable in managing male-predominant symptoms like impulsivity, distractibility, and rejection sensitivity and in improving relationships. This section explains how mind mapping can positively impact these issues.

- **Managing impulsivity and distractions:** The structured, web-like format of mind maps provides a contained visual space to capture our thoughts and ideas. This design can reduce the tendency for the mind to wander and get distracted. The very process of actively mapping out concepts anchors our attention and minimizes cognitive detours. For men with ADHD who often struggle with impulsive behavior and acting on every thought that arises, mind mapping offers a constructive outlet. Instead of blurting out ideas or acting hastily, we can simply map out those impulses in an organized manner within the mind map. This process of *downloading and organizing* can facilitate better self-regulation.

- **Self-regulation and rejection sensitivity:** Mind mapping's round ability to promote self-awareness and self-regulation is linked to us being able to represent our thoughts, emotions, and goals visually. This externalization of our cognitive processes can be incredibly insightful, allowing us to identify patterns, triggers, and areas that may require attention or improvement. Because we can often struggle with self-monitoring and emotional control, this heightened self-awareness is invaluable. Added to this, experiencing heightened rejection sensitivity or struggling with interpersonal challenges—a common challenge for men with ADHD—can be mitigated by using mind mapping as a self-regulation tool.

- **Relational improvements:** Effective communication and mutual understanding are necessary for healthy relationships.

For men with ADHD, communication challenges can often strain personal and professional connections. However, mind mapping offers a powerful solution by facilitating clear and organized expression of ideas and perspectives. The visual nature of mind maps provides a shared reference point, reducing misinterpretations and allowing for more coherent conversations. When collectively created with partners, family members, or colleagues, mind maps can also be used as a collaborative tool that facilitates understanding and problem-solving within relationships. They allow you to gain insight into each other's thought processes, concerns, and goals, promoting empathy, validation, and a deeper appreciation for differing perspectives.

• **Tailoring symptom management:** One of the most profound advantages of mind mapping is its adaptability. It allows us to tailor our approach to our unique strengths, preferences, and needs. Unlike rigid organizational methods, mind mapping encourages a personalized and creative approach to organizing thoughts and ideas. This is beneficial to men with ADHD as they often have diverse cognitive profiles and learning styles. While some may thrive on using keywords and succinct phrases, others may gravitate toward incorporating vivid imagery, symbols, and color coding. The integration of verbal (words) and nonverbal (images) elements creates a richly stimulating cognitive experience that caters to a wide range of processing preferences. In providing ourselves with a versatile and adaptable framework, we're able to customize our approach to symptom management by tapping into our strengths.

• **Integrating mind mapping into existing ADHD management strategies:** Because mind mapping is defined as a complementary tool, it can be combined with current ADHD management strategies to enhance the effectiveness of our treatment plan. Additionally, mind mapping is a powerful cognitive restructuring aid that allows us to visualize and challenge unhelpful thought patterns. The adaptability of mind mapping means we can integrate it into almost every area of our lives, using it to achieve our treatment goals and providing us with a more holistic approach to our symptom management.

• **Focus and attention:** One of the most significant advantages of mind mapping is its ability to enhance focus and attention. Visually externalizing thoughts and ideas using mind maps provides us with a structured canvas that helps anchor our cognitive processes. The web-like structure and use of keywords act as mental hooks, reducing the tendency for our minds to wander and facilitating sustained concentration.

• **Creativity enhancement:** Mind mapping stimulates increased creativity and problem-solving abilities. The free-flowing, nonlinear nature of mind maps encourages divergent thinking. It provides a way to explore new connections and associations between concepts, unlocking innovative solutions and fresh perspectives. When we use mind maps, we can tap into our unique creative potential, directing our thought processes and unlocking the innovative power of thinking outside the box.

Getting Started with Mind Mapping

We now know just how powerful mind mapping can be for men with ADHD, but if you are new to mind mapping, it's important to understand how to use this simple tool to unleash your full capabilities.

While this book has many exercises, you do not need to complete all of them. Instead, take the time to go through each chapter so that you can select the ones that are meaningful to you.

1. To begin with, you will need a blank canvas like a piece of paper,

whiteboard, digital mind mapping app, or the provided basic mind mapping template.

2. Start the mind map by drawing a central image or writing a key concept in the middle of your canvas. This will be the nucleus from which all other thoughts and ideas will radiate outward.

3. Take a moment and allow your mind to associate with this central concept freely. Place each thought on your mind map as a branch that stems from the central point. These branches can capture subtopics, keywords, or related ideas.

4. As you continue expanding your mind map, aim to use a single word or concise phrase for each new branch rather than add complete sentences. This approach mirrors how your brain naturally processes information—concise cues rather than dense blocks of text.

5. To prevent overthinking and maintain a free-flowing creative process, resist the urge to organize or categorize your ideas just yet. Instead, let your mind map grow organically, embracing the nonlinear nature of your thought patterns.

6. Once you've thoroughly explored and mapped out your central concept, step back and observe your map. Look for patterns, connections, and recurring themes.

7. You will now need to create actionable insights from your mind map. This can be done by first identifying the most prominent or well-developed branches. These may represent key areas of focus or priorities.

8. From there, you can begin to organize and categorize related ideas, extracting specific action steps, goals, or solutions. These elements are called subbranches and twigs.

Always remember that mind mapping is, by nature, a dynamic process. As we gain more experience using our mind maps, we may develop personalized mapping templates that could include color codes, symbols, or different organizational structures. These personalized mind maps are unique to us and resonate most with our brains. That is the beauty of mind mapping: It mirrors the natural inner workings of our brilliant, diverse brains.

Please note that the References section at the end of the book contains many useful links to mind map examples.

Basic Mind Map Template

This template explains the basic idea behind mind maps. On the next page, there is a blank one that you can use to complete the exercises throughout this book.

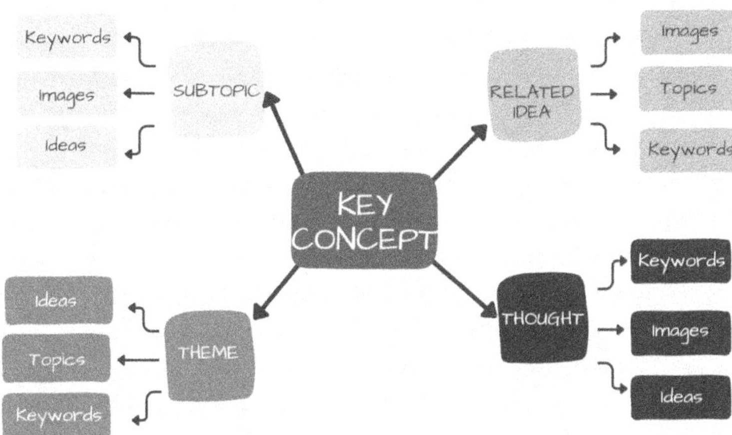

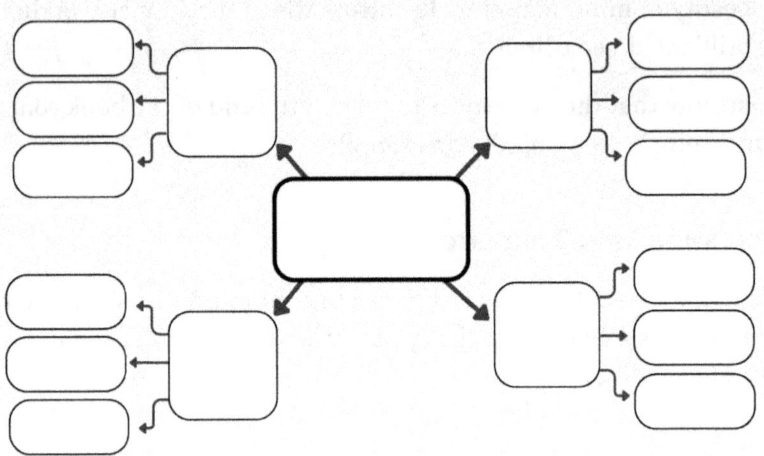

Chapter 2
Executive Functioning

Executive functioning is the cognitive processes that allow us to plan, organize, regulate our behavior, and achieve our goals. These higher-order brain functions act as an executive control system that governs our ability to manage our thoughts, emotions, and actions in pursuit of long-term objectives.

These executive skills are critical for navigating the demands of daily life and achieving our long-term goals. But we often forget to acknowledge the role executive functioning plays in seemingly small tasks like maintaining a tidy living space, following linear instructions, or nurturing healthy relationships. Deficits in executive functioning can severely hinder our capacity to take charge of our lives, leading to emotional distress, dysregulation, and sometimes even detachment from life.

The Impact of ADHD on Executive Functioning

ADHD directly affects our brain's executive functioning capabilities. Because ADHD involves a dysregulation of the frontal lobe regions of our brain, the condition impacts our higher-order cognitive processes, which include executive functioning skills like planning and organization as well as self-regulation (Leisman & Melillo, 2022).

For individuals with ADHD, executive function deficits often manifest as significant challenges across multiple domains in their lives. These manifestations can include:

- Time management difficulties like poor time awareness, chronic tardiness, and missing deadlines.

- Struggling to maintain order, losing items frequently, and disorganization in thoughts and physical spaces.

- Difficulties breaking down tasks into actionable steps to be taken for a positive outcome.

- Inattention to important tasks and being easily derailed by distractions.

- Trouble retaining information and forgetting instructions.

- Acting rashly without considering the consequences or impulsive behaviors.

- Emotional regulation issues like intense emotions, mood swings, or irritability.

- Task initiation difficulties that can present as severe procrastination and analysis paralysis—a condition in which over-thinking prevents action.

Of course, these executive functioning impairments can have far-reaching consequences, impacting our overall success in life. Ultimately, these behaviors frequently lead to low self-esteem, demoralization, and avoidant patterns in people with ADHD. Repeated encounters with failure because of our executive function deficits lead to a negative self-perception that can become a self-fulfilling prophecy, exacerbating existing challenges.

The Role of Mind Mapping in Enhancing Executive Functioning

As mind mapping is a dynamic visual tool that directly targets and supports several key executive functions, we can externalize our thoughts and break them down into an organized radial structure. It is a metaphorical scaffolding for higher-order cognitive skills that are often compromised in ADHD.

Let's break down each of these executive functioning deficits so that we can see how mind mapping can help us lay neurological pathways for better functioning.

- One of the primary executive deficits in ADHD is the *ability to formulate cohesive plans* to achieve goals. Mind mapping assists by allowing you to put out the overarching objective at the central point and then radiate outward into actionable subtasks and sequential steps.

- Men with ADHD often struggle with *impulsive behaviors* rooted in poor inhibitory control. Mind mapping combats this by providing a structured framework to slow down and organize your thoughts logically before acting rashly.

- A common issue for men with ADHD is difficulties with *working memory*—the ability to hold and manipulate information temporarily to complete tasks. Mind maps are incredibly powerful memory aids that integrate visual-spatial cues, associations, and miscellaneous representations of concepts. This multi-sensory coding enhances information encoding, storage, and retrieval.

Executive Functioning Mind Mapping Exercises

To complete these exercises, you'll need either a blank piece of paper, your preferred mind mapping software, or the provided template. You will also require a pen or pencil and colored markers/pencils to highlight key ideas and thoughts.

Make sure to follow the instructions and notes listed in Chapter 1, under "Getting Started with Mind Mapping," to help you organize your thoughts and gain key insights.

Each of the subsequent exercises will provide you with an objective plus additional instructions so that you know exactly why you're creating your mind map and what is required to formulate it.

Remember to walk away and return to your mind map with a fresh perspective if you're struggling to remain focused or become frustrated with the process. With time and practice, you will be able to complete an entire mind map more easily.

Exercise 1: Mind Map Your Daily Routine

Objective

This mind map helps you enhance your organization and time management skills by:

- Identifying priorities and essential tasks that require dedicated time and focus.

- Allocating time more effectively by visualizing the duration and sequence of activities.

- Recognizing potential time conflicts or overlaps that need to be resolved.

- Evaluating your use of time and developing a more structured, intentional approach to managing your daily schedule.

Instructions

1. Draw a central point or write "My Daily Routine" in the middle of your page.

2. Divide your day into broad time blocks, for example, morning, afternoon, and evening, by creating main branches drawn from the central point.

3. For each time block, create twigs to represent specific

    A. Tasks

    B. Appointments

C. Activities

4. To enhance visual organization, consider color coding different categories of activities—work, chores, self-care, leisure, and so on.

5. Draw branches for recurring tasks. Color code these in order of priority if you want to.

6. Identify and highlight essential, non-negotiable activities using bold colors, icons, or visual cues that draw attention. For example, a red question mark.

7. Once you've mapped out all components of your daily routine, step back and review the entire structure objectively. Look for potential time conflicts, inefficiencies, or areas that require better time allocation.

Here is a basic example of what the My Daily Routine mind map might look like.

Exercise 2: Mind Map Your Goals and Priorities

Objective

This mind mapping exercise is designed to help you clarify your goals and priorities by:

- Breaking down lofty, overwhelming goals into concrete, manageable steps.

- Identifying conflicts or connecting patterns between different goals.

- Enhancing planning and prioritization skills by defining timelines.

- Developing cognitive flexibility to adapt and reprioritize as needed.

Instructions

1. Draw a central point with a label such as "My Goals."

2. Draw main branches from this central point, each representing a key area of your life—career, health, relationships, personal growth, etc.

3. For each life area, generate twigs to define your specific

    A. Short-term goals

    B. Long-term goals

4. Once you have mapped out your goals, review them and identify which ones are most urgent or important to you at this stage. Highlight or emphasize these high-priority goals using visual cues like bolding, colors, or icons.

5. For your high-priority goals, generate additional subbranches to outline the key steps, milestones, or subgoals required to achieve them. Break larger goals down into manageable, actionable tasks.

6. Review your mind map and look for potential conflicts or patterns between different goals and tasks. Use cross-links, colors, or symbols to highlight these connections.

7. Finally, consider adding timeframes or deadlines for your goals and action steps using labels, annotations, or visual representations.

Exercise 3: Mind Map Your To-Do List

Objective

This mind mapping exercise helps you improve task prioritization, decision-making, and time management skills by:

- Distinguishing truly important tasks from distractions and prioritizing effectively based on urgency and significance.

- Reducing feelings of overwhelm by making thoughtful decisions on what to tackle immediately.

- Pinpointing potential areas of procrastination and creating countermeasures.

- Strengthening planning abilities by ordering and scheduling connecting tasks.

Instructions

1. Draw a central point with a label like "My To-Do List."

2. Draw main branches from the central point, each representing a broader category or context for your tasks, including

A. Work

B. Home errands

C. Any other relevant tasks

3. Under each main branch, list specific to-do items as twigs using concise labels or small images.

4. Review your listed tasks and identify which ones are

   A. Urgent and important

   B. Important but not urgent

   C. Urgent but not important

   D. Neither urgent nor important

5. Use a visual coding system, such as colors, shapes, or symbols to categorize tasks based on this importance–urgency principle.

6. Add emphasis to urgent and important tasks by bolding or high-lighting the twigs.

7. Evaluate potential connections or conflicts between tasks using cross-links, referencing, or visual cues to highlight relationships.

8. Consider integrating temporal markers like due dates, timeframes, or sequencing numbers to convey deadlines and order.

9. Review the full map and identify areas that seem overwhelming or may benefit from further breakdown into smaller steps.

Exercise 4: Mind Map a Work Task or Assignment

Objective

This mind mapping exercise aims to enhance your planning, organiza-tion, and creative skills for effective project and task management by:

- Boosting creativity through open-ended brainstorming and idea generation.

- Organizing thoughts and materials into a cohesive, logical structure.

- Prioritizing tasks based on importance and criticality, and breaking down complex projects into actionable, sequential steps.

- Identifying potential roadblocks, risks, or resource needs up front.

- Improving time management by scheduling and allocating timeframes.

Instructions

1. Draw a central point representing the core work task, project, or assignment using a concise label.

2. Draw main branches from this point, each depicting a key area, milestone, or phase of the project.

3. Under each main branch, create twigs to map out specific phases for

A. Components

B. Activities

C. Materials needed

4. For the research and/or idea-gathering phase, create a dedicated branch for open-ended brainstorming.

5. Once you have exhausted idea generation, review and organize your brainstormed thoughts into meaningful categories or topics using colors, symbols, or visual boundaries.

6. Using priority reminders, map out the logical sequencing of project phases, milestones, and deliverables.

7. Integrate time management by mapping out deadlines and targets, as well as scheduling using date notations or visual representations of timeframes.

8. Review and refine the mind map, identifying potential complications or resource needs.

9. Adjust as needed.

Exercise 5: Mind Map Strategies for Managing Impulsivity

Objective

This mind mapping exercise helps cultivate greater self-awareness around impulsive behavioral patterns while proactively developing adaptive coping mechanisms by:

- Identifying high-risk contexts for impulsive reactions and unhelpful thought patterns.

- Generating an arsenal of cognitive and behavioral tools for self-regulation, distinguishing proactive strategies from reactive interventions.

- Connecting your values and goals as motivators for self-control.

- Enhancing preparedness and responsiveness to impulsive urges.

Instructions

1. Draw a central point with a label such as "Managing Impulsivity."

2. Draw main branches from your central point, each representing a common situation or context where you tend to struggle with impulsive behaviors like

   A. Social situations

   B. Decision-making

   C. Spending

   D. Communication

3. Under each situational branch, using concise labels or visuals, list specific impulsive behaviors, unhelpful thought patterns, or triggers that tend to arise.

4. Once you have mapped out your impulsive tendencies, create additional twigs to depict coping strategies, interventions, or alternative responses for each scenario.

5. Consider using different colors, shapes, or visual cues to differentiate proactive strategies from reactive ones.

6. Integrate reminders of your core values, long-term goals, or consequences that can serve as motivators for self-control using symbols or imagery.

7. Look for potential connections between impulsive contexts and strategies that may work across multiple situations.

8. Review and refine your mind map, identifying areas needing additional strategizing or tools.

9. Download your free bonus to learn how to better control your impulsive behavior with the ABC Model!

https://selftransformationpath.com/BundlePB
You can also scan this QR code to get access.

Mind mapping can be a powerful tool for strengthening the executive functioning abilities that ADHD often negatively impacts. Regular mind mapping benefits extend to enhancing planning and prioritization skills and boosting creativity and decision-making. As mind maps provide a versatile visual-spatial framework to support higher-order cognitive processes, you can begin to manage the symptoms of executive functioning deficits better.

Chapter 3

Emotional Regulation

Emotional intelligence is the ability to sense, understand, and effectively apply the power and acumen of emotions as a source of human energy, information, connection, and influence.

Robert K. Cooper

Men with ADHD can often find themselves held back by their emotions. The same neurological differences that shape how we process information and maintain focus can also impair our ability to modulate our emotional responses.

Intense emotional surges of frustration, anger, anxiety, or impulsive outbursts are common experiences for us. Our heightened emotional states can not only impact our inner psyche but also disrupt relationships, decision-making capabilities, and our overall quality of life.

At the core of these emotional regulation issues lies a fundamental component of ADHD: decreased neurological inhibition. This causes the brain mechanisms responsible for putting on the brakes and moderating our behaviors, impulses, and emotional reactivity to be compromised. Consequently, we can unknowingly lean toward emotional dysregulation.

The Impact of ADHD on Emotional Regulation Skills

Men with ADHD often present more outward symptoms and have difficulty inhibiting their impulses, not just behaviorally but emotionally as well. We can experience intense emotional surges and outbursts that happen almost reflexively with little cognitive control over the reaction. This impulsive emotional hyperactivity makes it very difficult to pause, reflect, and choose an appropriate response.

In essence, men with ADHD experience a knee-jerk reaction instead of stopping to think and take action. Furthermore, the inattentive symptoms of ADHD can impair emotional self-awareness, making it difficult to recognize others' emotional cues. We can get locked into our emotions through hyperfocus or even tune out emotional information as we fight the sensory and emotional overload within us.

The combination of executive dysfunction, inhibitory control problems, attentional deficits, and sensory processing challenges creates the perfect storm inside us. We need to find ways to manage this storm if we're to discover some form of emotional balance within ourselves.

The Role of Mind Mapping in Supporting Emotional Regulation

Mind mapping offers a powerful visual-spatial approach to help you develop self-awareness, self-reflection, and emotional mastery. With mind mapping, you can:

- Begin to develop emotional intelligence by recognizing your internal emotional states, identifying emotional and external triggers, and creating a personalized emotions vocabulary that will help you manage how you feel.

- Facilitate self-reflection and recognize patterns in your emotions as well as any physical sensations you may experience while they are passing. This will also allow you to analyze any emotional historical patterns you have so that you can find the root cause of your feelings.

- Identify triggers and develop preemptive strategies for moments when you experience overwhelming emotions. Once you identify your triggers, you can begin to develop effective coping strategies and become emotionally prepared.

- Monitor your progress and the development of your emotional regulation skills so that you can properly activate your brain's reward centers. Validating your progress and assessing which areas need a little more improvement puts you firmly in control of your emotional regulation improvement journey.

Emotional Regulation-Specific Mind Mapping Exercises

Exercise 6: Mind Map Your Emotional Triggers

Objective

This mind map provides you with a comprehensive, multi-layered exploration of your unique emotional triggers and associated patterns by:

- Gaining deeper self-awareness around specific trigger situations and events.

- Recognizing underlying emotions, bodily sensations, and cognitive distortions (see the Glossary for more information).

- Developing tailored coping strategies and regulation protocols for each trigger.

- Revealing connections between diverse triggers to generalize strategies.

Instructions

1. Draw a central point with a label like "My Emotional Triggers."

2. Draw main branches from the central point, each depicting a broad category where you commonly experience emotional triggers—work, relationships, sensory stimuli, etc.

3. Under each category branch, list specific trigger situations or events twigs using concise labels or images.

4. Once triggers are mapped out, create additional twigs from each trigger, depicting any underlying emotional responses sparked by that trigger. These should be marked as "Cognitive Sensations".

5. Add other twigs to map out any physical sensations you notice when triggered. Mark these twigs as "Physical Sensations."

6. More twigs should be added to the "Cognitive Sensations" twigs for unhelpful thought patterns or stories that get activated.

7. Look for connections between triggers that activate similar underlying emotions or patterns. Use cross-links or boundaries to show these relationships.

8. Identify any areas on the map that appear to be underexplored. These may indicate emotional blind spots that need further investigation.

9. Create a separate branch to map out more constructive, planned coping strategies and interventions for each core trigger category.

Exercise 7: Mind Map Your Support Network

Objective

This mind map provides a panoramic view of your current emotional support system while reminding you that you're not alone in dealing with hardships. You will be:

- Gaining an appreciation for existing supportive relationships across your life in various contexts.

- Identifying opportunities to deepen or reciprocate supportive connections.

- Revealing personal strengths through your capacity to provide support to others.

- Pinpointing contexts where new supportive relationships could be cultivated.

Instructions

1. Draw a central point representing yourself, using your name or initials.

2. Draw main branches from this central point, each one representing a different domain of your life. This could include family, friends, workplace, community, or online spaces.

3. Draw twigs under each life domain, depicting emotional support and encouragement from

   A. Individuals

   B. Groups

   C. Resources

4. Use names, initials, images, or icons to represent each supportive connection.

5. For each person or resource included, create additional twigs highlighting

   A. The type of support they provide. For example, accountability, emotional, financial, and so on

   B. Any specific strengths or qualities that make their support meaningful

   C. How you can reciprocate and provide support to them

6. Use colors, symbols, or other visual metaphors to denote the relative strength, closeness, or importance of different supportive connections.

7. Look for any domains where supportive connections seem to be missing entirely. Emphasize these as areas to cultivate new supportive relationships.

8. Use flowcharts or paths to show interconnections between different supportive spheres of your life.

9.Highlight any relationships or resources that could benefit from being nurtured, strengthened, or activated for increased support.

Exercise 8: Mind Map Your Stress Management Strategies

Objective

This mind mapping exercise allows you to build a repository of stress management strategies tailored to your unique needs and preferences. You will be:

- Identifying personal favorite relaxation and regulation strategies and understanding why they are effective.

- Revealing strategies that mutually reinforce each other, and highlighting areas where you may need more variety or new strategies.

- Building resilience by diversifying your regulating and coping toolkit.

- Promoting self-care with inspirational reminders and affirmations.

Instructions

1. Draw a central point in the middle of your page and label it "My Stress Management."

2. Draw main branches from the central point, each depicting a different category of stress management strategy. These can include

    A. Physical

    B. Mental

    C. Emotional

    D. Sensory

    E. Social environmental

3. Under each category branch, draw twigs listing specific stress-relieving activities, practices, or techniques.

4. Once you've exhausted your list of strategies, review the map and highlight or use color coding to emphasize your personal favorites.

5. Write additional branches detailing why each preferred strategy is effective for you, how it makes you feel, the benefits you experience, and so on.

6. Identify any strategies that target multiple categories. Use cross-links or boundaries to show these interconnections.

7. Look for any categories that seem to be missing stress-relief techniques you'd like to explore further.

8. Create a separate branch to list potential new strategies you'd like to incorporate into your routine.

9. Finally, consider adding a branch for personal reminders, affirmations, or inspirational quotes related to resilience and self-care.

Exercise 9: Mind Map Your Emotional Goals

Objective

This mind map allows you to construct a detailed plan for achieving meaningful emotional wellness goals by:

- Ensuring your goals are specific, actionable, and realistic.

- Aligning goals with your bigger vision of emotional well-being.

- Prioritizing your goals and tracking incremental progress within set timelines.

- Identifying areas of synergy between goals for combined objectives.

Instructions

1. Draw a central point representing your vision of emotional wellness and balance.

2. Draw main branches from your central point, each depicting a key aspect of emotional well-being you'd like to focus on, e.g. reduce stress levels, increase gratitude.

3. For each emotional wellness branch, create twigs listing specific goals you want to work toward.

4. Once you have mapped out your goals, review them and identify two or three highest priority goals to tackle first. Denote these using visual emphases like bolding or highlights.

5. For each high-priority goal, create additional twigs, breaking the objective down into actionable, measurable steps/milestones or SMART goals (see the Glossary for more information).

6. Integrate temporal markers like timelines, deadlines, or timeframes for completing each actionable step using date labels or visual representations.

7. Look for connections between goals or parallels in the actionable steps.

8. Create a section listing potential resources, books, apps, communities, or individuals that could support your goal pursuits.

9. Create a new branch to include motivational quotes, affirmations, or visual metaphors to inspire continued devotion to your emotional growth process.

Exercise 10: Mind Map Your Positive Affirmations

Objective

This affirmation mind map provides a vibrant, comprehensive collection of empowering beliefs and self-supportive statements you can use to help motivate yourself and counteract negative self-talk by:

- Reinforcing accurate, positive self-perceptions by high-lighting personal strengths and accomplishments.

- Cultivating self-compassion and self-acceptance.

- Strengthening self-confidence and personal agency.

- Building emotional resilience and inner peace.

Instructions

1. Draw a central point representing your highest self. You can use an empowering word, mantra, or symbolic image.

2. Draw main branches from this central point, each depicting a key area of your life. This can include your

    A. Relationships

    B. Career

    C. Health

    D. Personal growth

3. Using concise, powerful statements under each life area branch, add twigs with positive affirmations related to that branch.

4. Use vibrant colors, emotional imagery, and different fonts to make the affirmations vivid and resonant.

5. Include affirmations expressing self-compassion, inner strength, and belief in your abilities under relevant branches.

6. Create other branches with higher-level affirmations about your wholeness, inherent worth, and spiritual essence.

7. Make a branch for listing traits, accomplishments, or experiences that instill you with positive self-regard.

8. Review and highlight the most empowering, grounding affirmations.

Exercise 11: Mind Map Your Emotion Regulation Toolkit

Objective

This mind map creates a personalized collection of the tools that resonate most with you for emotional regulation and de-escalation of *big* emotions by:

- Creating an accessible visual reference during dysregulated moments.

- Aligning categorized strategies for your specific emotional challenges.

- Using inspirational mantras and success logs to boost self-regulation beliefs and track effective strategies.

- Building a dynamic, continually evolving resource as you develop new skills.

Instructions

1. Draw a central point titled "My Regulation Toolkit" or a symbolic representation.

2. Draw main branches for different categories of regulation strategies that can include:

A. Grounding techniques—deep breathing, muscle relaxation, mindfulness

B. Cognitive-behavioral strategies—reframing, neutralizing thoughts

C. Physical and sensory activities—exercise, listening to music, crafting

D. Environmental interventions—dimming lights, aromatherapy

E. Interpersonal support—calling a friend, counseling hotlines

3. Under each branch, draw twigs to list specific techniques, resources, or activities using concise labels.

4. Add visual icons, colors, or graphics to differentiate strategies that help with different situations.

5. Highlight your personal favorite or most effective strategies.

6. Integrate a branch with instructions or reminders for strategically using the toolkit.

7. Create a branch for logging successful strategies used to reinforce self-efficacy beliefs.

8. Leave space to add new strategies as you continue expanding your regulation skills.

For men with ADHD, emotional regulation can be tough. It can demand a lot of patience, self-compassion, and an unwavering commitment to personal growth. Using mind mapping as a tool to help explore, label, and manage emotions provides hope and a solid foundation for living a more emotionally balanced life.

Chapter 4
Social Well-Being

The richest human beings are those who have managed to enrich others.

Marjorie Hinckley

For many adult men with ADHD, navigating the nuances of social interaction and relationship building can be immensely challenging. The reasons for our strained social interactions vary but primarily revolve around our inability to sustain attention and our impulsivity. Regardless of why we battle with social connections, our symptoms can present significant obstacles for us.

In group settings, impulsive speaking, interrupting others, and struggling to read social cues can lead to awkward silences and people avoiding us. During one-on-one conversations, the attentional issues symptomatic of ADHD may lead to our focus drifting. This can make it appear as if we're distracted, aloof, or rude when this is not our intention.

How ADHD Affects Relationships and Social Interactions

As ADHD involves dysregulation of executive brain functions, social interactions, and, more specifically, relationship building, it can be challenging for us. While each of us has specific social symptoms, these outward manifestations of our ADHD can vary wildly. From social anxiety and avoidance to risk-taking behavior and volatile, unhealthy attachments, ADHD can pose significant social challenges that we need to explore so that we understand them better.

- Impulsive communication patterns, which can manifest as

disinhibited speech, can cause our conversations to derail and be a major hurdle for us.

• Distractibility and attention lapses make it very difficult for us to remain focused on what other people are saying.

• Executive dysfunction symptoms can make it hard for us to monitor our conversations and emotions, follow through with commitments and promises, and properly resolve conflicts within a relationship.

• Social cue interpretation can also be particularly challenging for us as we may find it difficult to read facial expressions, body language, and vocal tones.

• Rejection sensitivity can build as we frequently experience social rejection, judgment, or misunderstandings.

While ADHD undoubtedly creates obstacles for us, we can overcome them when we mind map our areas of weakness and tailor specific solutions to help support our social interactions.

The Role of Mind Mapping in Facilitating Healthy Relationships

While the neurocognitive profile of ADHD can cause us relationship issues, mind mapping provides innovative ways to cultivate self-awareness, develop and strengthen our communication skills, and build the empathy required for healthy relationships.

The first step to nurturing fulfilling social bonds is developing insight into how our ADHD manifests outward, specifically when it comes to our social interactions. Mind mapping allows us to visually explore and articulate our emotional experiences, cognitive distortions, attachment styles, and social needs. This self-mapping process strengthens our emotional vocabulary and self-understanding as a foundation for healthy relationships with ourselves and others.

Furthermore, mind maps enable us to prepare for conversations thoughtfully by allowing us to map out our perspectives, goals, and potential obstacles. Thus, we can create mind maps that help us develop proper speech patterns and remind us to be attentive to body language and pause before reacting.

Social Well-Being Mind Mapping Exercises

Exercise 12: Mind Map Your Communication Style

Objective

This mind map provides you with the ability to self-assess your unique communication tendencies, strengths, and growth areas by:

- Heightening your self-awareness around communication skills and identifying weaknesses and patterns that persist across communication contexts.

- Exploring self-talk, emotions, and physiological influences.

- Prioritizing development targets for enhanced interpersonal skills.

- Incorporating supportive strategies aligned with your motivations and goals.

Instructions

1. Draw a central point representing yourself communicating with others and label it "My Communication Style."

2. Draw main branches representing key areas where you communicate. For example

    A. One-on-one

B. Groups

C. Public speaking communications

3. Under each area, create twigs listing your strengths as a communicator in those situations.

4. Add separate twigs detailing your weaknesses or areas for improvement in each area.

5. Look for patterns in your mind map—are certain strengths or weaknesses consistent across contexts? Use boundaries and/or colors to denote these.

6. Create branches exploring your general communication preferences. This could be

A. Verbal

B. Written

C. Through listening

7. Include personal reflections, typical thought patterns, or physical experiences that influence your communication.

8. Create a branch highlighting particularly impactful communication skills you'd like to develop further.

9. Integrate supportive strategies, affirmations, or visual cues related to mindful communication practices.

Exercise 13: Mind Map Your Social Goals

Objective

This mind map provides a detailed roadmap for achieving elevated social growth and relationship-building by:

- Constructing an inspiring vision of your social potential.

• Proactively strategizing for predictable vulnerabilities and
pitfalls.

• Setting structured timelines and accountability for consistent
practice.

• Continually updating the mind map as goals are reassessed
and adjusted.

Instructions

1. Draw a central point with an image representing your vision for
social enrichment and connectivity, or label it "My Social Goals."

2. Draw main branches from your central point depicting key areas
where you want to build social skills and bonds.

3. Under each area branch, draw twigs mapping out specific goals you
want to work toward using concise labels or visuals.

4. Conduct a goal-priority analysis defining which two or three goals
demand immediate focus. Make sure to emphasize these visually.

5. For each high-priority goal, map out incremental action steps as
twigs using verbs like

   A. Attend the networking meeting on Monday at 5 p.m.

   B. Volunteer to present sales meeting

   C. Offer assistance in organizing a social get-together

6. Create branches listing potential obstacles, triggers, or vulnerabilities that often derail your social efforts.

7. Map out tailored strategies, including

   A. Preventative practices

   B. Affirmations for addressing each vulnerability

C. Classes, skills, or resources that can be used to improve social etiquette

8. Look for parallels on your mind map and assess which strategies could be used across multiple goals.

9. Set realistic timelines and deadlines for your mapped goals and steps using date labels.

Exercise 14: Mind Map Your Social Boundaries

Objective

This mind map provides a comprehensive expression of your personal boundaries across emotional, physical, and social areas of your life by:

- Solidifying your awareness and intentionality around your personal boundaries.

- Distinguishing context-specific boundaries from broader life categories.

- Integrating affirmations for asserting boundaries self-assuredly.

- Outlining communication scripts so that you can express your boundaries clearly.

Instructions

1. Draw a central point representing your personal boundaries, values, or limits. Label this "My Boundaries."

2. Draw main branches from your central point depicting key domains of boundaries. These should include your

A. Emotional boundaries

B. Physical boundaries

C. Social boundaries

3. Under the emotional boundaries, branch twigs that list specific boundaries related to your

A. Feelings and vulnerabilities

B. Need for privacy or space

C. Comfort with emotional intimacy

D. Expectations for emotional support

4. For the physical boundaries branch, depict limits around your

A. Personal space and touch

B. Bodily autonomy and consent

C. Physical safety and security

D. Privacy and territorial boundaries

5. Look for any boundaries represented in multiple areas and visually integrate them, showing their multifaceted nature.

6. Use colors, images, and symbols to capture the essence and emotions associated with each boundary.

7. Create branches with affirmations for asserting your boundaries confidently and compassionately.

8. Consider adding a branch with sample scripts or phrases to convey key boundaries.

9. Include a branch that lists out specific tools and behaviors that help reinforce your boundaries, self-respect, and values.

Exercise 15: Mind Map Your Usual Social Anxiety or Avoidance Patterns

Objective

This mind map aims to help you identify and understand your common patterns of social anxiety and avoidance by:

- Gaining clarity on the specific triggers and contexts that provoke anxiety or avoidance.

- Recognizing the thoughts, beliefs, and self-talk that fuel your social anxiety, and the emotional and physical symptoms that accompany your anxious responses.

- Exploring the avoidance behaviors and safety behaviors you rely on to cope with social discomfort and their consequences.

- Setting the stage for developing alternative coping strategies and challenging anxious thoughts.

Instructions

1. Draw a central point representing your social anxiety and avoidance patterns. Label this "My Social Anxiety and Avoidance."

2. Draw main branches from your central point for the key domains of your social anxiety experience, such as

A. Triggering situations and contexts

B. Anxious thoughts and beliefs

C. Emotional and physical symptoms

D. Avoidance and safety behaviors

3. For example, under the "Triggering situations" branch, draw twigs depicting specific social contexts, interactions, or performance situations that typically provoke anxiety for you, like

    A. Meeting new people

    B. Speaking up in class or meetings

    C. Attending social events

    D. Being the center of attention

    E. Asserting needs or boundaries

4. Do the same for the "Anxious thoughts and beliefs" branch, writing down common thoughts or self-talk you experience when anxious.

5. Under the "Emotional and physical symptoms" branch, note the feelings and bodily sensations that you experience when socially anxious.

6. Under the "Avoidance and safety behaviors" branch, identify the actions you take to avoid or minimize anxiety in social situations.

7. Draw connecting lines between branches to illustrate how the different domains of your social anxiety interact and reinforce each other.

8. Include a branch for methods that relieve your anxiety in the short term.

9. Include a branch for long-term consequences of your anxiety and avoidance patterns.

10. Review your completed mind map with curiosity and compassion, validating the very real challenges of social anxiety.

Exercise 16: Mind Map Your Empathy and Understanding

Objective

This mind map helps you enhance your empathy skills, perspective-taking abilities, and emotional intelligence in social interactions by:

- Identifying situations where you struggle to empathize with others.

- Recognizing personal biases or judgments that create a roadblock in your relationships.

- Cultivating compassion and kindness toward yourself and others.

- Developing more meaningful, connected relationships through empathy, active listening (see the Glossary for more information) and validation techniques.

Instructions

1. Draw a central point representing empathy and understanding. Label this "Empathy and Understanding."

2. Create main branches for key areas of focus that include

    A. Active listening skills

    B. Perspective-taking techniques

    C. Managing biases

    D. Becoming curious and open-minded

    E. Practicing compassion for others

3. Under each main branch, create twigs to explore specific strategies, techniques, or prompts for key empathy skills, such as

    A. Pushing yourself out of your comfort zone

    B. Getting feedback on behaviors

    C. Examining others' perspectives with curiosity

    D. Learning to ask open questions

4. Include a branch for real-life situations where you can practice these skills.

5. Add twigs to list the benefits of strengthening empathy.

6. Make sure to leave blank branches to modify or add new tasks as your empathic skills improve so that you can cover any blind spots identified.

Exercise 17: Mind Map Your Conflict Resolution Strategies

Objective

This mind map aims to develop effective conflict resolution skills, promote open communication, and strengthen your relationships with healthy communication by:

- Identifying your typical conflict response style (see the Glossary for more information): avoidance, accommodation, competition, compromise, or collaboration.

- Recognizing triggers or patterns that contribute to conflicts.

- Learning to manage emotions and maintain respect during conflicts by practicing active listening and effective communication techniques.

- Building resilient, healthy relationships through proactive conflict resolution.

Instructions

1. Draw a central point representing your conflict resolution ideals. Label this "Conflict Resolution Strategies."

2. From your central point, draw main branches for focus areas, including

A. Understanding my conflict styles

B. Identifying triggers and patterns

C. Effective communication techniques

D. Emotional regulation

3. Under each main branch, draw twigs that explore specific strategies and techniques of conflict resolution. Take the following into consideration:

A. Using "I" statements (see the Glossary for more information)

B. Uncovering trigger delay strategies

C. Problem-solving skills

D. Emotional regulation techniques

4. Include a branch for real-life conflicts where you can practice these strategies or ask a partner, family member, friend, or coworker to practice with you.

5. Create a blank space to modify or add new tasks as your empathic skills improve so that you can cover any blind spots identified.

Exercise 18: Mind Map Your Social Engagement Plan

Objective

This mind map aims to help you identify social activities, events, or groups to participate in, set intentions for social interaction, and overcome barriers to social engagement by:

• Clarifying your social needs, preferences, and values.

• Identifying interests or hobbies that can foster social connection.

• Exploring different types of social activities or events to participate in.

• Creating an action plan for a consistent, fulfilling social connection.

Instructions

1. Draw a central point representing your social engagement aspirations. Label this "Social Engagement Plan."

2. Draw branches from your central point for key areas of focus, including

    A. Identifying social needs and preferences

    B. Exploring interests and hobbies

    C. The types of social activities and events you enjoy

    D. The barriers you experience when engaging with others, etc.

3. Under each main branch, draw twigs that explore your social needs, interests and hobbies, and social activities goals.

4. Include twigs for specific people, communities, or resources that can support your social engagement goals.

5. Create a separate branch that outlines an action plan with SMART goals you can set to implement your social engagement plan.

6. Review your mind map often so that you can identify any obstacles you may have faced and outline strategies that have worked.

Social connection and belonging are fundamental human needs that can be challenging for men with ADHD. However, this doesn't mean we cannot overcome our neurological deficits to build long-lasting, meaningful relationships in our lives. By using the provided mind mapping exercises, we can develop empathy, set boundaries, and resolve conflicts in a healthy way that promotes resilience and emotional intelligence.

Chapter 5

Overthinking and Intrusive Thoughts

The greatest weapon against stress is our ability to choose one thought over another.

William James

We are no strangers to the constant barrage of thoughts, worries, and mental chatter that happens in our heads. But, when left unchecked, these thoughts and worries can become overwhelming and exhausting.

In addition to the usual chatter in our brains, overthinking and intrusive thoughts are common challenges that can make it difficult to focus, complete tasks, and find inner peace. These racing thoughts can range from minor worries to persistent, anxiety-inducing ruminations that interfere with our daily lives.

How ADHD Affects Thought Management

Our symptoms are at the core of our tendency to struggle with thought management. We must understand exactly how these symptoms manifest when it comes to overthinking and intrusive thoughts if we're going to use mind mapping effectively to counteract and manage our symptoms.

- One of the biggest obstacles to managing our thoughts is our diminished ability to control our impulses. This manifests in difficulty regulating our thought patterns, especially when they're negative or intrusive, leading to a tendency to fixate on and overthink certain ideas.

● Even if we try to focus on positive or productive thoughts, we can easily become distracted by invasive worries or mental tangents. This can lead to a constant state of mental juggling, where we struggle to maintain a coherent train of thought.

● Finding the sustained attention needed to redirect our thoughts and maintain focus on a different mental track can be challenging. The mental fatigue that comes with constantly battling intrusive thoughts can make it difficult to continue redirecting our mental energy.

● As we know, ADHD impairs key executive functions like emotional regulation, attentional control, and cognitive flexibility. This can make it incredibly difficult to manage our thought patterns, regulate our emotional responses to intrusive thoughts, and shift our mental gears when needed.

● For men with ADHD, the constant influx of mental stimuli, both external and internal, can be overwhelming. This mental noise can drown out attempts at rational thought, making it difficult to focus on and manage the desired thought patterns.

● The inability to self-regulate plays a significant role in exacerbating our intrusive thoughts. When we struggle to control our impulses, emotions, and attention, it becomes incredibly challenging to redirect our mental energy away from negative or unproductive thought patterns.

Understanding these unique neurological barriers is the first step toward overcoming them. When we recognize that our ADHD fuels our thoughts, we can create mind maps that highlight targeted strategies to help us overcome the chatter in our minds.

The Role of Mind Mapping in Balancing Thoughts

Mind mapping mirrors the information in our brains in a structured way that helps bring order to the mental chaos in our minds. Visually organizing our thoughts and uncovering our self-limiting beliefs and critical patterns can help us challenge the intrusive thoughts that keep us trapped in negative spirals.

When using mind mapping, we can categorize our thoughts into different branches or themes. This allows us to separate productive thoughts from intrusive ones and prioritize our mental energy accordingly. This includes:

- **Trigger identification:** Mind maps can help us identify the triggers that lead to overthinking and intrusive thoughts.

- **Pattern recognition:** As we create mind maps of our thoughts over time, we can begin to recognize patterns in our thinking.

- **Coping strategy development:** Mind mapping can be a powerful tool for brainstorming and organizing coping strategies for managing overthinking and intrusive thoughts.

- **Progress tracking:** As we implement these coping strategies, we can use mind maps to track our progress and evaluate the effectiveness of different techniques.

Incorporating mind mapping into our thought management routine can help reduce the power of intrusive thoughts and promote a more balanced, intentional way of thinking. Some specific benefits of using mind maps for managing overthinking and intrusive thoughts include improved metacognition, better mental flexibility, awareness of our problem-solving ability, and reduced anxiety. All of this leads to greater self-confidence and feelings of self-efficacy as we begin to gain control over our thought processes.

Mind Mapping Exercises for Overthinking and Intrusive Thoughts

Exercise 19: Mind Map Your Thought Patterns

Objective

This mind map aims to increase self-awareness of thought patterns, identify cognitive distortions, and challenge irrational beliefs by:

- Gaining insight into your mental habits and tendencies.

- Recognizing thought patterns that contribute to overthinking and intrusive thoughts.

- Identifying cognitive distortions, such as all-or-nothing thinking, catastrophizing, or overgeneralization.

- Developing strategies for challenging and reframing irrational beliefs.

Instructions

1. Begin with a central point representing your thought patterns. Label it "My Thought Patterns."

2. Draw main branches from your central point for recurring themes in your thoughts, for example

A. Self-criticism

B. Self-doubt

C. Worries about the future

3. Under each main branch, draw twigs for specific examples of these thought patterns in your daily life. Include the triggers that often precipitate these thoughts and the emotions they evoke.

4. Create a separate branch for cognitive distortions you notice in your thought patterns, such as, "I'm not good enough." Label each distortion and provide examples of how it manifests in your thinking.

5. Draw a branch for strategies to challenge and reframe irrational beliefs. This might include techniques like cognitive restructuring, examining evidence, or considering alternative perspectives.

6. Include a branch for positive affirmations and self-talk that you can use to counter negative thought patterns and cultivate a more balanced outlook.

7. Review your mind map regularly to deepen your self-awareness, catch thought patterns early, and practice challenging irrational beliefs in the moment.

Exercise 20: Mind Map Your Worry List

Objective

This mind map aims to help you externalize worries, prioritize concerns, and develop strategies for addressing worries effectively so you can focus on the following:

- Gaining a clear overview of the issues that are occupying your mental space, distinguishing between productive concerns and unproductive rumination.

- Identifying the root causes and triggers of your worries.

- Prioritizing worries based on their importance and your ability to control or influence them.

- Developing action plans for addressing legitimate concerns and practicing letting go of worries that are outside your control or not serving you.

Instructions

1. Begin with a central point representing your worries. Label this "My Worry List."

2. Draw main branches from your central point for different categories of worries, including

> A. Health and well-being

> B. Relationships and social connections

> C. Work and career

> D. Finances and material security

> E. Personal growth and self-actualization

3. Under each main branch, draw twigs for specific worries or concerns you have in that area. Be as detailed and honest as possible.

4. Create a separate branch for evaluating your worries. Based on its importance and urgency, assign each worry a priority level.

5. Draw a branch for action steps and problem-solving strategies. For example, drawing up a pros and cons list.

6. Include a branch for coping strategies and self-care practices that can help you manage the emotional impact of worries and reduce overall stress levels.

7. Review your worry list mind map regularly, updating it as new concerns arise. Celebrate your progress as you successfully address and let go of worries.

Exercise 21: Mind Map Your Mindfulness Practice

Objective

This mind map is designed to help you create present-moment awareness, increase mindfulness, and reduce rumination and mental clutter by:

• Developing a personalized toolkit of mindfulness strategies that resonate with your needs and preferences.

• Establishing a regular mindfulness routine to support mental well-being.

• Increasing your capacity for present-moment awareness and nonjudgmental observation.

• Reducing the frequency and intensity of overthinking and intrusive thoughts.

Instructions

1. Begin with a central point representing your mindfulness practice. Label this "My Mindfulness Practice."

2. Draw main branches from your central point for different categories of mindfulness practices, including

A. Meditation and breathwork

B. Body awareness and relaxation

C. Sensory grounding techniques

E. Mindful movement and exercise

D. Gratitude and self-compassion practices

3. Under each main branch, draw twigs for specific techniques or exercises you want to incorporate into your mindfulness practice.

4. Create a separate branch for your mindfulness routine. Outline when, where, and how often you will engage in mindfulness practices.

5. Draw a branch for obstacles and challenges you anticipate in maintaining your mindfulness practice.

6. Brainstorm strategies for overcoming these barriers and staying committed.

7. Keep your mindfulness mind map visible and refer to it often as a reminder of your commitment to present-moment awareness and mental well-being.

Exercise 22: Mind Map Your Positive Affirmations

Objective

This mind map helps you counter negative self-talk, cultivate self-compassion, and foster a positive mindset to balance overthinking by executing these points:

- Developing a repertoire of positive self-talk to replace negative inner dialogue.

- Cultivating self-compassion and kindness toward yourself to boost your self-confidence and self-worth.

- Reframing limiting beliefs and expanding your sense of possibility.

- Creating a visual reminder of your strengths, values, and aspirations.

Instructions

1. Draw a central point representing your positive mindset. Label this "My Positive Affirmations."

2. Draw main branches from your central point for different categories of affirmations, such as

    A. Self-love

    B. Confidence

    C. Resilience

    D. Growth

3. Under each main branch, draw twigs for your favorite affirmations.

4. Include a branch for affirmations that specifically counter your most common negative self-talk patterns and limiting beliefs.

5. Draw a branch for ways to integrate these affirmations into your daily life.

6. Review your positive affirmations mind map regularly, especially when you experience negative self-talk or overthinking patterns.

Exercise 23: Mind Map Your Relaxation Techniques

Objective

This mind map is designed to help you develop a personalized toolkit for relaxation, promoting relaxation response, and reduce physiological arousal by:

- Identifying relaxation practices that resonate with your needs, creating a go-to resource for self-soothing.

- Reducing physical tension and promoting a sense of calm.

- Developing proactive strategies for coping with stress and preventing burnout.

- Prioritizing self-care and relaxation as essential components of mental health.

Instructions

1. Draw a central point representing your relaxation toolkit. Label this "My Relaxation Techniques."

2. Draw main branches from your central point for different categories of relaxation techniques, including

A. Breathing exercises

B. Progressive muscle relaxation

C. Guided imagery

D. Mindfulness and meditation practices

E. Creative expression

F. Nature-based relaxation

3. Under each main branch, draw twigs for specific techniques, exercises, or resources you want to explore and incorporate into your relaxation practice.

4. Create a separate branch for the techniques that work best for you from the list generated in Step 3.

5. Draw a branch for relaxation reminders and cues you can use throughout your day to prompt a relaxation response.

6. Include a branch for relaxation mantras or affirmations that promote a sense of calm and ease.

7. Place your relaxation techniques mind map in a prominent location and refer to it regularly, especially during times of high stress or anxiety.

Exercise 24: Mind Map Your Distraction Strategies

Objective

This mind map aims to help you interrupt overthinking patterns, redirect attention, and engage in alternative activities to break the cycle of rumination by:

- Developing a toolkit of healthy distractions to use when overthinking arises.

- Identifying activities that fully engage your attention and provide a sense of flow.

- Cultivating hobbies and interests that promote a sense of joy and accomplishment.

- Creating a go-to list of alternative thought patterns and perspectives to explore.

Instructions

1. Draw a central point representing your distraction strategies. Label this "My Distraction Techniques."

2. Draw main branches from your central point for different categories of distraction techniques, including

A. Exercise

B. Creativity and hobbies

C. Social connection

D. Mentally-engaging tasks and puzzles

E. Learning and skill-building

F. Volunteer work and acts of kindness

3. Under each main branch, draw twigs for specific activities, ideas, or resources you want to explore and incorporate into your distraction toolkit.

4. Draw a branch for environmental cues and reminders you can use to prompt a shift in attention, like inspirational quotes, uplifting images, or meaningful objects.

5. Keep your distraction strategies mind map easily accessible and refer to it whenever you find yourself stuck in a pattern of overthinking or rumination.

Exercise 25: Mind Map Your Gratitude Journal

Objective

This mind map will help you cultivate an attitude of gratitude, shift focus from negative thoughts to positive experiences, and promote emotional well-being by:

- Developing a consistent gratitude practice that reinforces positive thinking patterns, even amidst challenges.

- Counterbalancing negative bias and overthinking with a focus on what is going well, enhancing your overall sense of contentment, joy, and life satisfaction.

- Cultivating resilience and coping skills by anchoring in gratitude during difficult times.

- Deepening your appreciation for the people, experiences, and small pleasures that enrich your life.

Instructions

1. Draw a central point representing your gratitude practice. Label this "My Gratitude Journal."

2. Draw main branches from your central point for different categories of gratitude, such as

A. Relationships and social support

B. Personal strengths

C. Material comforts

D. Nature

E. Experiences

F. Health and well-being

G. Spiritual connections

3. Under each main branch, draw twigs for specific people, things, experiences, or moments you are grateful for.

4. Create a separate branch for gratitude practices and rituals you want to incorporate into your daily life.

5. Draw a branch for gratitude affirmations and mantras that reinforce your commitment to a grateful mindset.

6. Include a branch for the benefits and positive outcomes you have experienced or hope to experience through your gratitude practice.

7. Place your gratitude mind map in a prominent location and refer to it daily.

Overthinking and intrusive thoughts are common challenges for adult men with ADHD. The constant mental chatter, racing thoughts, and persistent worries can be exhausting and overwhelming, impacting mental well-being, productivity, and overall quality of life.

Mind mapping, however, is a powerful tool for bringing order and clarity to your mental landscape. Visually organizing your thoughts allows you to gain insight into your thinking patterns, identify triggers and cognitive distortions, and develop targeted strategies for managing mental chatter.

Chapter 6

Overwhelm, Fear Of Rejection, And Rejection Sensitivity

The greatest mistake you can make in life is to continually fear you will make one.

Elbert Hubbard

Rejection is a painful and often overwhelming experience for anyone, but for adult men with ADHD, the emotional impact can be particularly intense. Many of us struggle with rejection sensitivity, which is a heightened emotional response to real or perceived rejection that can lead to feelings of deep hurt, anger, and even shame. This sensitivity can make even minor instances of rejection, like a friend canceling plans or a coworker disagreeing with our ideas, feel like a crushing blow to our self-worth.

The fear of missing out (FOMO) is another common challenge for men with ADHD, and it can exacerbate our rejection sensitivity. The constant worry that we'll be left out or excluded from social events, professional opportunities, or important relationships can put us on high alert for any signs of rejection. This hypervigilance can lead to emotional dysregulation, where we struggle to manage our intense emotional reactions and may lash out or withdraw in response to perceived disregard.

How ADHD Affects Interpretation of Rejection and Formation of Rejection Sensitivity

ADHD can significantly influence the way we interpret and respond to rejection. It's important to understand how these symptoms contribute to the formation of rejection sensitivity so that we can develop effective strategies for managing this painful emotional pattern.

- Impulsivity can manifest as a tendency to react quickly and intensely to emotional triggers. When we perceive rejection, we may impulsively lash out in anger, withdraw in shame, or make rash decisions to protect ourselves from further hurt.

- ADHD can make it difficult for us to regulate our emotions effectively. We may struggle to modulate the intensity of our feelings or shift our emotional gears when needed. This emotional dysregulation can cause us to magnify the significance of perceived rejection, turning minor slights into major catastrophes in our minds.

- Men with ADHD are highly sensitive to criticism, even when it's constructive or well-intentioned. They may interpret feedback or disagreement as a personal attack or a sign that they're fundamentally flawed.

- ADHD can impact our ability to read and interpret social cues accurately. We may miss subtle signs of acceptance or misinterpret neutral interactions as rejecting.

The formation of rejection sensitivity in people with ADHD is often a complex interplay of developmental experiences and cognitive processes. Many of us have a history of social struggles, academic challenges, and complex family dynamics related to our ADHD symptoms. These early experiences of feeling different, misunderstood, or criticized can lay the foundation for a heightened sensitivity to rejection.

The Role of Mind Mapping in Balancing Rejection Sensitivity and Overwhelm

Mind mapping helps us gain clarity, perspective, and emotional balance when we need to deal with rejection. When we can visually organize our thoughts and feelings, it becomes easier for us to untangle the complicated emotions we feel when receiving criticism or rejection. Mind mapping provides us with a framework to:

- Create structure and clarity out of our thoughts when we feel sensitive or overwhelmed by criticism.

- Reframe our negative thoughts and biases that often fuel our fear of rejection.

- Identify our rejection sensitivity and overwhelm triggers so that we can better manage our responses.

- Develop coping strategies for moments when we feel over-whelmed by our feelings.

- Become self-reflective and gain insights into others' perspectives as well as the thoughts and emotions we feel.

- Pause before we react to rejection and allow the rational and cognitive centers of our brains to catch up with what has happened.

In essence, harnessing the power of mind mapping allows us to transform our relationship with rejection sensitivity and overwhelm. We move from a place of reactivity and suffering to one of understanding, resilience, and emotional balance.

Mind Mapping Exercises for Managing Rejection Sensitivity and Overwhelm

Exercise 26: Mind Map Your Triggers

Objective

This mind map aims to increase self-awareness of triggers, identify patterns, and develop strategies for managing emotional reactions by:

- Gaining clarity on the specific contexts and experiences that provoke painful emotions.

- Recognizing common themes or patterns in your triggers, developing insight into the underlying fears, beliefs, or past experiences that fuel your reactions.

- Identifying early warning signs and subtle cues that a trigger is present.

- Setting the stage for developing proactive coping strategies and self-care practices.

Instructions

1. Draw a central point representing your triggers. Label this "My Triggers."

2. Draw main branches from your central point for the key categories of triggers in your life, including

A. Relationships and social situations

B. Work and performance contexts

C. Family dynamics and interactions

D. Personal vulnerabilities and fears

3. Under each main branch, draw twigs to identify specific situations, events, or thoughts that tend to trigger feelings of rejection or overwhelm.

4. Draw twigs next to each trigger to note the emotional reactions and physical sensations that arise, such as anger, shame, anxiety, or a racing heartbeat.

5. Draw connecting lines between triggers that share similar themes, fears, or beliefs. This can help you identify patterns and underlying vulnerabilities.

6. Include a branch for early warning signs or subtle cues that a triggering situation may be developing, such as a knot in your stomach or an urge to withdraw.

7. Create a branch for proactive coping strategies and self-care practices that can help you manage your emotional reactions and navigate triggering situations more effectively.

8. Review your completed mind map with curiosity and nonjudgment, acknowledging the wisdom and resilience in your reactions.

Exercise 27: Mind Map Your Self-Compassion

Objective

This mind map helps cultivate self-compassion, challenges self-critical thoughts, and builds resilience in the face of rejection or overwhelm. You will be:

- Developing a kinder, more supportive inner dialogue, reframing perceived failures or setbacks as opportunities for growth and learning.

- Affirming your inherent worth and value, independent of external validation.

- Building emotional resilience and coping skills for navigating painful experiences.

- Deepening your capacity for self-love, self-care, and self-acceptance.

Instructions

1. Draw a central point representing your self-compassion. Label this "My Self-Compassion."

2. Draw main branches from your central point for the key domains of self-compassion:

A. Mindfulness

B. Common empathy

C. Self-kindness

3. Under the "Mindfulness" branch, include statements or affirmations that validate your emotional experience.

4. Under the "Common empathy" branch, add reminders that people are imperfect and that it's normal to make mistakes.

5. Under the "Self-kindness" branch, include compassionate and supportive messages.

6. Draw additional twigs for self-care practices, soothing activities, or supportive people and resources.

7. Include twigs for the benefits and positive outcomes of practicing self-compassion.

8. Place your self-compassion mind map in a prominent location and refer to it regularly, especially in moments of self-doubt or self-criticism.

Exercise 28: Mind Map Your Confidence

Objective

This mind map aims to help you identify areas in your life where you feel confident and do not have feelings of overwhelm by:

- Recognizing your strengths, skills, and achievements.

- Identifying supportive relationships and environments that boost your self-assurance.

- Celebrating how you already embody confidence and self-trust and discovering patterns and strategies that you can apply to build confidence in other areas.

- Cultivating a sense of pride and self-appreciation for your unique qualities and accomplishments.

Instructions

1. Draw a central point representing your confidence. Label this "My Confidence."

2. Draw main branches from your central point for the key domains in which you feel confident, including your

> A. Relationships and social connections.
>
> B. Work, talents, and skills.
>
> C. Hobbies and passions.
>
> D. Personal qualities and values.
>
> E. Self-care and well-being practices.

3. Under each main branch, draw twigs with specific examples of your confidence in that area, e.g., accomplishments and successes you've achieved, challenges you've overcome, or skills you've mastered.

4. Include twigs for the supportive people, resources, or environments that contribute to your confidence.

5. Draw connecting lines between different domains or experiences to highlight common threads or transferable skills that show confidence.

6. Create a branch for the positive qualities and self-beliefs that emerge from your experiences of confidence.

7. Add a branch for how you can apply the lessons and strategies from your confident areas to build self-assurance in dimensions you feel less secure in or more prone to overwhelm.

8. Refer to your confidence mind map often, especially when you're facing self-doubt or venturing into new challenges.

Exercise 29: Mind Map Your Self-Confidence Goals

Objective

This mind map aims to create a roadmap to increase all-around self-confidence to mitigate rejection sensitivity or thoughts of preemptive rejection. You will be:

- Clarifying your aspirations for personal growth and self-assurance.

- Identifying resources, support systems, and strategies to help you build confidence.

- Creating a visual representation of your progress and accomplishments.

- Developing a proactive, empowered approach to building self-confidence.

Instructions

1. Draw a central point representing your self-confidence goals. Label this "My Self-Confidence Goals" or draw a representation of self-confidence.

2. Draw main branches from your central point for the key areas of your life where you'd like to increase confidence, including

   A. Social settings and interactions

   B. Personal relationships and dating

   C. Work and professional development

   D. Self-expression and assertiveness

   E. Body image and self-acceptance

3. Under each main branch, draw twigs identifying specific goals or milestones that represent increased confidence, including

A. Initiating conversations with new people

B. Expressing needs and boundaries clearly in relationships

C. Taking on leadership roles or projects at work

D. Speaking up and sharing ideas in group settings

E. Practicing self-compassion and body positivity

4. Break down each goal into SMART goals that you can work on incrementally.

5. Add a branch for resources, support systems, or strategies that can help you achieve your confidence goals.

6. Include a branch for potential obstacles or challenges you may face in pursuing your goals, and brainstorm strategies for overcoming these barriers. You can use your mind map from Exercise 34 for this.

7. Create a branch for celebrating your progress and accomplishments along the way. List rewards or self-acknowledgments you'll give yourself for reaching milestones or demonstrating increased confidence.

8. Review and update your self-confidence mind map regularly, acknowledging your growth and adapting your goals as needed.

Exercise 30: Mind Map Your Coping Strategies

Objective

This mind map aims to help you develop a personalized toolkit for emotional regulation, stress reduction, and self-soothing during challenging times by:

- Identifying healthy, effective ways to navigate difficult emotions and experiences.

- Creating a diverse range of self-care tools and techniques to support your well-being.

- Developing a proactive approach to managing stress and building resilience.

- Prioritizing your emotional health and well-being as a foundation for thriving.

Instructions

1. Draw a central point representing your coping strategies. Label this "My Coping Strategies."

2. Draw main branches from your central point for different categories of coping strategies, including

    A. Mindfulness and stress reduction techniques

    B. Emotional self-care and self-soothing activities

    C. Social support and connection

    D. Physical self-care and wellness practices

    E. Creative expression and outlets

3. Under each main branch, add twigs for specific tools, techniques, or activities that you find helpful for managing stress and difficult emotions. These could include deep breathing exercises, meditation, journaling, etc.

4. Include twigs for specific steps or instructions for implementing each coping strategy, as well as any resources or materials you need.

5. Draw connecting lines between coping strategies that work well together or support similar goals.

6. Create a branch for proactive self-care routines or rituals you can practice regularly to build resilience and maintain emotional well-being.

7. Add a branch for coping strategies or self-care practices that you'd like to try or explore further, and include steps for incorporating them into your life.

8. Keep your coping strategies mind map readily accessible and refer to it often, especially during times of stress or overwhelm.

Exercise 31: Mind Map Your Growth Mindset

Objective

This mind map aims to foster a growth mindset, embrace challenges, and view rejection or overwhelm as an opportunity for growth and learning by:

- Cultivating a more adaptable, resilient approach to challenges and setbacks by reframing failures or rejections as valuable learning experiences.

- Embracing effort, persistence, and incremental progress as keys to success.

- Developing a love of learning and a willingness to step outside your comfort zone.

- Building self-efficacy and a belief in your capacity for growth and change.

Instructions

1. Draw a central point representing your growth mindset. Label this "My Growth Mindset," or draw a growth mindset.

2. Draw main branches from your central point for key principles of a growth mindset, including

A. Embracing challenges and stepping outside your comfort zone

B. Viewing failures or setbacks as opportunities for learning and growth

C. Focusing on effort, persistence, and incremental progress

D. Cultivating a love of learning and a willingness to try new things

E. Seeking out feedback and constructive criticism as tools for improvement

F. Celebrating the journey of personal development, not just the destination

3. Under each main branch, add twigs for specific affirmations, beliefs, or reminders that support that aspect of a growth mindset, like, "Challenges help me grow and develop new skills."

4. Include twigs for specific strategies or practices you can use to cultivate a growth mindset in the face of rejection or overwhelm.

5. Draw twigs for role models, mentors, or success stories who inspire you and exemplify the power of a growth mindset.

6. Create a branch for the benefits and positive outcomes you've experienced or anticipate experiencing by adopting a growth mindset.

7. Add a branch for growth mindset mantras or quotes that you find particularly motivating or inspiring and that you can turn to in moments of self-doubt or frustration.

8. Display your growth mindset mind map in a prominent place and refer to it often, especially when facing challenges or setbacks.

These mind maps will help you develop a comprehensive toolkit for managing your feelings of rejection and overwhelm. Setting self-confidence goals and developing coping strategies allows you to clarify boundaries and cultivate a growth mindset. This can help you overcome your feelings of overwhelm by building self-awareness, self-compassion, and self-confidence.

Chapter 7

Time Management, Procrastination, and Analysis Paralysis

Time is the most valuable thing a man can spend.

Theophrastus

Time management is a constant challenge for everyone with ADHD. As men, however, society places less pressure on us compared to women to be punctual, which can lead to bad habits forming around our time management. The very nature of ADHD, with its difficulties in executive functioning, makes managing time effectively a complex and multifaceted issue. From planning and prioritization to time estimation and procrastination, the hurdles we face can seem insurmountable at times.

How ADHD Affects Time Management and Procrastination

One of the core difficulties lies in our ability to plan and prioritize effectively. With ADHD, it can be challenging to break down larger tasks into manageable steps, estimate the time each step will take, and create a realistic action plan. We may find ourselves overwhelmed by the sheer number of tasks on our to-do list, struggling to determine which ones are truly important and which can wait.

This difficulty with prioritization can lead to a phenomenon known as analysis paralysis: the tendency to get stuck in the planning phase, endlessly weighing options and possibilities without actually taking action. Thus, we may find ourselves spending hours researching the perfect time management system or agonizing over the optimal order in which to complete tasks, only to find that the day has slipped away without any tangible progress.

Procrastination is another common challenge for men with ADHD, and it can have a profound impact on our productivity and goal attainment. The tendency to put off tasks, especially those that are boring, difficult, or anxiety-provoking, can lead to a cycle of last-minute rushes, missed deadlines, and chronic stress. We may find ourselves consistently underestimating the time required for tasks, leading to overscheduling and a constant sense of being behind.

The Role of Mind Mapping in Enhancing Time Management and Overcoming Procrastination

Mind mapping is a powerful tool for bringing structure, clarity, and visual organization to time management strategies and task planning. By creating a visual representation of tasks, deadlines, and priorities, we can gain a clearer understanding of what needs to be done and develop a realistic plan of action.

- One of the key benefits of mind mapping for time management is the ability to break down large, complex tasks into smaller, more manageable steps.

- Mind maps can be an effective tool for setting and visualizing deadlines. By adding timeline branches to our task map, we can create a clear visual representation of when each step needs to be completed.

- Mind mapping can help us transform our task lists into a concrete, actionable plan. Visually organizing our tasks and priorities allows us to identify the specific steps needed to move forward and overcome procrastination.

- When we're stuck in the planning phase, endlessly weighing options and possibilities, mind mapping can help us get unstuck by forcing us to commit our ideas to paper.

- Mind maps help us identify and prioritize tasks so we can make informed decisions about where to focus our time and energy.

- As we work through our tasks and projects, mind mapping can help us track our progress and stay motivated. Visually marking off completed tasks and milestones can create a sense of momentum and accomplishment.

Mind Mapping Exercises for Time Management, Procrastination, and Analysis Paralysis

Exercise 32: Mind Map Your Daily Schedule

Objective

This mind map is designed to enhance time awareness, prioritize tasks, and allocate time effectively using mind mapping techniques. You will be:

- Gaining a clear overview of your daily commitments and responsibilities.

- Identifying potential conflicts or overlaps in your schedule.

- Prioritizing tasks based on urgency and importance, and allocating realistic time blocks for each activity.

- Discovering opportunities for optimizing your time usage.

Instructions

1. Draw a central point representing your daily schedule. Label this "My Daily Schedule."

2. Draw main branches from your central point for different time

segments of your day. You can use your mind map from exercise 1 in chapter 2 to help speed this up.

A. Morning

B. Afternoon

C. Evening

3. Under each main branch, add twigs for specific appointments, tasks, or activities you need to complete during that time segment, e.g., work meetings, deadlines, family commitments, etc.

4. Include twigs for the estimated time durations of each task or activity to help you allocate your time realistically and avoid over-booking yourself.

5. Draw connecting lines between related tasks or activities that can be grouped or completed in sequence to optimize your time usage.

6. Create a branch for potential obstacles or time-wasters that may disrupt your schedule, such as procrastination, distractions, or unexpected interruptions.

7. Brainstorm strategies for minimizing or overcoming these challenges.

8. Add a branch for buffer time or white space in your schedule to allow for flexibility, rest, and self-care.

9. Review your daily schedule mind map regularly, both at the beginning of the day to set your intentions and priorities and at the day's end to reflect on your progress and make adjustments for the future.

Exercise 33: Mind Map Your Task Prioritization

Objective

This mind map helps improve task prioritization skills, focus on high-impact activities, and reduce procrastination by:

• Clarifying which tasks and projects are most critical, and identifying ones that can be delegated, deferred, or eliminated.

• Allocating your time and energy to the highest-leverage activities.

• Developing a strategic, proactive approach to managing your workload.

• Increasing your sense of control and accomplishment in your daily life.

Instructions

1. Draw a central point representing your task prioritization. Label this "My Task Prioritization."

2. Draw four main branches from your central point, labeling them

A. Urgent and important

B. Not urgent but important

C. Urgent but not important

D. Not urgent and not important

3. Under each branch, add twigs for specific tasks, projects, or responsibilities that fall into that category.

4. Include deadlines, time estimates, or resource requirements for each task to help you plan and allocate your time effectively.

5. Draw connecting lines between tasks that are related or dependent on each other, indicating the sequence or hierarchy of your priorities.

6. Create a branch for strategies or habits you can focus on that are often the most neglected but also the most critical for long-term success and fulfillment.

7. Add a branch for tasks you can delegate, automate, or eliminate to free up more time and energy for your highest-priority activities.

8. Review your task prioritization mind map regularly, ideally at the beginning of each week or month, to align your daily activities.

Exercise 34: Mind Map Your Procrastination Triggers

Objective

This mind map is designed to increase self-awareness of procrastination habits, understand underlying motivations, and develop strategies for overcoming procrastination by:

- Gaining insight into the emotional, cognitive, and situational factors that contribute to your procrastination.

- Recognizing common thoughts, beliefs, or self-talk that reinforce procrastination.

- Creating targeted strategies for addressing specific procrastination triggers.

- Building self-awareness and self-regulation skills to help you stay focused and motivated.

Instructions

1. Draw a central point representing your procrastination triggers. Label this "My Procrastination Triggers."

2. Draw main branches from your central point for different categories of procrastination triggers, including

A. Emotional triggers

B. Cognitive triggers

C. Situational triggers

D. Physiological triggers

E. Social triggers

3. Under each main branch, add twigs for specific examples or instances of these triggers in your own life.

4. Include any thoughts, beliefs, or self-talk that typically accompany each trigger, such as, "I'm not good enough to do this."

5. Draw connecting lines between triggers that often occur together or reinforce each other, indicating patterns or cycles of procrastination.

6. Create a branch for strategies or techniques you can use to address each type of trigger. You can use your previous mind maps for this.

7. Add a branch for self-care practices or mindset shifts that can help you build resilience and overcome procrastination in the long term.

8. Review your procrastination triggers mind map regularly, especially when you find yourself struggling to stay focused or motivated. Use your insights to develop targeted interventions and experiment with different strategies until you find what works best for you.

Exercise 35: Mind Map Your Analysis Paralysis Triggers

Objective

This mind map helps uncover the thoughts driven by fear and how you can overcome paralyzing fear by:

- Identifying the thoughts and decisions you have caught in a thought loop.

- Challenging these thoughts with logic and reason.

- Developing confidence in your decision-making ability.

- Making decisions and taking action using the insights from exercises 33 and 34.

Instructions

1. Draw a central point representing your analysis paralysis triggers. Label this "My Analysis Paralysis Triggers."

2. Draw main branches from your central point for different categories of decisions or situations that often trigger analysis paralysis, such as

   A. Career or business decisions

   B. Financial decisions

   C. Relationship or personal decisions

   D. Health or lifestyle decisions

3. Under each main branch, draw twigs for specific examples of decisions or thoughts that have you caught in a loop.

4. Include any underlying fears or limiting beliefs that contribute to your analysis paralysis.

5. Draw connecting lines between triggers that share similar fears or thought patterns, indicating common themes or areas for growth.

6. Create a branch for strategies or techniques to challenge fear-based thoughts and make decisions more effectively.

7. Add a branch for affirmations or reminders that can help you trust your intuition, take calculated risks, and embrace the learning opportunities that come with making decisions.

8. Review your analysis paralysis triggers mind map regularly, especially when you find yourself stuck in indecision or overthinking. Use your insights to identify patterns, challenge limiting beliefs, and practice decision-making more confidently and clearly.

Exercise 36: Mind Map Your Decision-Making Process

Objective

This mind map helps you clarify decision-making factors, weigh up pros and cons, and make informed decisions to overcome analysis paralysis by:

- Gaining a comprehensive view of the factors influencing your decision.

- Identifying and prioritizing your values, goals, and objectives.

- Exploring and evaluating the risks and benefits of different options.

- Developing a structured, logical approach to decision-making.

Instructions

1. Draw a central point representing the decision you need to make. Label this with the specific decision or question you are facing.

2. Draw main branches from your central point for the key factors or criteria you need to consider in making your decision, such as

A. Financial implications

B. Personal or professional growth opportunities

C. Alignment with values and long-term goals

D. Risk tolerance and potential downsides

E. Timing and logistics

3. Under each main branch, draw twigs for specific details, data points, or considerations related to them.

4. Create a branch for generating and exploring different options or alternatives, like "Accept the job offer" or "Negotiate for better terms."

5. For each option, draw twigs to map out the potential short-term and long-term consequences, both positive and negative. Use "+" and "-" symbols or different colors to visually distinguish between the pros and cons.

6. Draw connecting lines between options and criteria to indicate which factors are most relevant or influential for each path forward.

7. Create a branch for your preliminary decision or top choice based on your analysis. Include any remaining questions, concerns, or action steps needed to move forward confidently.

8. Review your decision-making mind map regularly throughout the decision-making process, updating it with new information or insights as needed.

Exercise 37: Mind Map Your Time-Blocking Strategy

Objective

This mind map optimizes time usage, minimizes distractions, and increases productivity through focused, time-bound work sessions by:

- Creating a visual, easily referenced guide for your daily or weekly personal and professional schedule.

- Prioritizing high-impact work and protecting time for deep focus.

- Building momentum and motivation by completing tasks within dedicated time blocks.

- Developing a more realistic, sustainable approach to productivity and time management.

Instructions

1. Draw a central point representing your time-blocking strategy. Label this "My Time-Blocking Strategy" or draw a representation of structuring your time.

2. Draw main branches from your central point for different categories of tasks or activities you want to allocate time for, such as

    A. Deep work or high-priority projects

    B. Shallow work or routine tasks

    C. Meetings and communication

D. Personal and self-care activities

3. Under each main branch, draw twigs for specific tasks, projects, or activities that fall into that category, like "Write project proposal" under the "Deep work" branch or "Respond to emails" under the "Shallow work" branch.

4. Assign a specific time block or duration to each task or activity based on its complexity, importance, and your natural energy levels throughout the day. You could use the Pomodoro Technique to help you with this (see the Glossary for more information).

5. Create a branch for breaks, rest, and recovery time, including short breaks between time blocks and longer restorative activities.

6. Draw connecting lines between tasks or time blocks that are related or dependent on each other, indicating your day's optimal sequence or flow.

7. Add a branch for potential obstacles or distractions that could disrupt your time-blocking strategy.

8. Brainstorm strategies for minimizing or overcoming these challenges, like setting clear boundaries or using website blockers.

9. Include a branch for tracking and reviewing your progress, noting tasks completed, time spent, and any adjustments needed to optimize your time-blocking approach.

10. Review your time-blocking mind map at the beginning of each day or week, using it as a visual guide and reminder of your priorities and commitments.

Exercise 38: Mind Map Your Reflection and Review Process

Objective

This mind map allows you to develop continuous improvement, learn from past experiences, and refine time management and productivity techniques over time by:

- Cultivating a growth mindset and embracing learning opportunities.

- Identifying patterns, strengths, and areas for improvement in your productivity habits.

- Celebrating your achievements and milestones and building motivation and momentum.

- Adapting your strategies and techniques based on what works best for you.

Instructions

1. Draw a central point representing your reflection and review process. Label this "My Reflection and Review Process."

2. Draw main branches from your central point for different areas or domains you want to reflect on, including

A. Time management and productivity techniques

B. Goal setting and progress toward objectives

C. Work-life balance and personal well-being

D. Relationships and communication

3. Under each main branch, add twigs for specific questions or prompts to guide your reflection, like "What worked well this week in terms of managing my time and energy?"

4. Create a branch for capturing key learnings, insights, or *aha* moments that emerge from your reflection process.

5. Draw connecting lines between different areas of reflection to highlight patterns and themes.

6. Add a branch for setting intentions, goals, or action steps based on your reflections. Break down larger intentions into SMART goals to help you stay focused and accountable.

7. Include a branch for self-compassion and gratitude, acknowledging your efforts, progress, and resilience even in the face of setbacks or challenges.

8. Schedule regular time for reflection and review, whether daily, weekly, or monthly. Use your mind map as a guide and record of your ongoing growth and development.

While time management and overcoming procrastination can feel like a challenge, it's important to remember that change is possible. Incorporating mind mapping techniques into your planning and prioritization strategies means you can begin to break free from the cycle of analysis paralysis and procrastination so that you can take purposeful action toward your goals.

Chapter 8

Dealing With ADHD Learning Disabilities and Comorbid Conditions

Strength does not come from winning. Your struggles develop your strengths. When you go through hardships and decide not to surrender, that is strength.

Arnold Schwarzenegger

Men with ADHD can find navigating the challenges of daily life to be complex and overwhelming: However, for those who also face comorbid learning disabilities and mental illnesses, the difficulties can be even more difficult.

Comorbidity means the presence of two or more disorders in the same person and is remarkably common with ADHD. Among adult men with ADHD, some of the most common comorbid conditions include anxiety disorders, depression, and anger dysregulation.

When ADHD co-occurs with other conditions, it can exacerbate symptoms, complicate treatment approaches, and create a unique set of obstacles that require specialized understanding and support.

Depression is another frequent comorbidity that can compound the feelings of frustration, self-doubt, and helplessness that many men with ADHD experience. The lack of motivation, energy, and interest associated with depression can make it challenging to engage in the very strategies and activities that could help manage ADHD symptoms, creating a vicious cycle of inaction and despair.

How ADHD Affects the Brain Structure and Common Comorbid Conditions

To effectively manage ADHD and its comorbid conditions, it's essential to understand how ADHD affects brain structure and function. Exploring the neurological underpinnings of ADHD symptoms, as well as the common co-occurring disorders, helps us develop a more comprehensive and targeted approach to our treatment and support.

- The imbalances in key neurotransmitters, particularly dopamine and norepinephrine, play a crucial role in regulating attention, impulse control, and motivation. In men with ADHD, there may be deficiencies or inefficiencies in the production, release, or uptake of these neurotransmitters.

- The frontal lobes, particularly the prefrontal cortex, are responsible for executive functions like planning, organization, and self-regulation. In men with ADHD, an underactivity or underdevelopment in these regions may contribute to difficulties with task initiation, goal-directed behavior, and inhibitory control.

- The limbic system, which includes structures like the amygdala and hippocampus, is involved in emotional processing and regulation. In men with ADHD, there may be hyperactivity or dysregulation in these regions, leading to heightened emotional reactivity, mood swings, and difficulty with emotional self-control.

- Anxiety disorders are among the most common comorbid conditions in people with ADHD. The constant worry, fear, and rumination associated with these disorders can exacerbate ADHD symptoms, making it even harder to focus, prioritize, and take action.

- Oppositional defiance disorder (ODD) is characterized by a pattern of angry, irritable, and defiant behavior toward authority figures. This can include arguing, refusing to comply with rules, and deliberately annoying others. In men with ADHD, emotional regulation issues can present as ODD. Added to this, overstimulation and feeling overwhelmed can compound ODD behaviors as we defiantly avoid certain tasks to prevent feeling overstimulated.

• ADHD often co-occurs with specific learning disabilities, like dyslexia, dyscalculia, and dysgraphia. These disorders can further exacerbate the academic challenges associated with ADHD as individuals struggle to process, retain, and apply information in specific domains.

The Role of Mind Mapping in Managing Comorbid Conditions and Building Neural Pathways

Mind mapping can be used to manage the symptoms of comorbid conditions, improve executive functioning, and promote neuroplasticity. Visually organizing information, breaking down complex challenges, and developing targeted action plans mean mind mapping can help reduce overwhelm, increase clarity, and facilitate the development of new neural pathways for adaptive functioning.

• Mind mapping can be an effective strategy for managing the symptoms of comorbid conditions, including anxiety, depression, and anger dysregulation.

• Emerging research suggests that mind mapping may have the potential to promote neuroplasticity, or the brain's ability to form fresh neural connections and adapt to new experiences.

• The process of creating and engaging with mind maps can help build new neural pathways for adaptive functioning. Repeatedly practicing breaking down complex information, organizing ideas visually, and developing targeted action plans can strengthen the cognitive processes underlying executive function, emotional regulation, and problem-solving.

• Mind mapping can be a powerful tool for brainstorming and organizing coping strategies for managing the symptoms of comorbid conditions. The visual nature of the mind map can make it easier to remember and access these strategies in moments of need, promoting a sense of self-efficacy and control.

It's important to note that mind mapping is not a standalone solution for managing ADHD and comorbid conditions. Instead, it is a complementary tool to be used in conjunction with other evidence-based treatments, such as medication, therapy, and lifestyle interventions. However, mind mapping can be a valuable addition to any comprehensive treatment plan as it harnesses the power of visual thinking and neuroplasticity.

Mind Mapping Exercises for Comorbid Conditions

Exercise 39: Mind Map Your Anxiety Triggers

Objective

This mind map helps you increase your awareness of specific triggers that contribute to anxiety symptoms, allowing for better recognition and management of anxiety-inducing situations by:

• Gaining clarity on the specific contexts and experiences that trigger your anxiety, recognizing common themes or patterns.

• Identifying early warning signs and subtle cues that a trigger is present.

• Developing self-compassion and insight into the underlying fears, beliefs, or past experiences that fuel your reactions.

• Setting the stage for developing proactive coping strategies and self-care practices.

Instructions

1. Draw a central point representing your anxiety triggers. Label this "My Anxiety Triggers."

2. Draw main branches from your central point for different categories of anxiety triggers, including

> A. Social situations

> B. Work or school pressures

> C. Health concerns

> D. Financial stressors

> E. Relationship conflicts

3. Under each main branch, draw twigs for specific examples of triggers within that category.

4. Draw connecting lines between triggers that are related or often occur together, indicating patterns or themes in your anxiety experiences.

5. Include a branch for any physical sensations, thoughts, or emotions that typically accompany your anxiety triggers, like a racing heart.

6. Create a branch for any coping strategies or techniques that have helped you manage specific triggers in the past.

7. Review your anxiety triggers mind map regularly, using it as a tool for self-awareness and proactive anxiety management.

Exercise 40: Mind Map Your Physical Anxiety Symptoms

Objective

This mind map lets you compile a comprehensive list of physical symptoms that may be triggering behaviors like impulsiveness, fidgeting, and avoidance by:

• Gaining a clear overview of the bodily sensations and experiences associated with your anxiety.

• Recognizing the interconnectedness of physical symptoms and anxious behaviors.

• Identifying patterns and triggers in your physical anxiety experiences.

• Setting the stage for selecting targeted coping strategies for symptom relief.

Instructions

1. Draw a central point representing your physical anxiety symptoms. Label this "My Physical Anxiety Symptoms."

2. Draw main branches from your central point for different areas of the body where you tend to feel anxiety symptoms, including

A. Head and face

B. Chest and heart

C. Stomach and digestive system

D. Muscles and limbs

E. Skin—for temperature regulation

3. Under each main branch, add twigs for specific physical symptoms you experience in that area. These can include headaches, clenched jaw, dizziness, and so on.

4. Draw connecting lines between symptoms that often occur together or seem to trigger one another, indicating patterns or cascades of physical anxiety responses.

5. Include a branch for noting any behavioral changes or impulsive actions that may be triggered by these physical symptoms.

6. Create a branch for coping strategies or self-care practices that can help alleviate specific physical symptoms.

7. Review your physical anxiety symptoms mind map regularly, using it as a tool for body awareness and targeted symptom management.

Exercise 41: Mind Map Your Coping Strategies for Anxiety

Objective

This mind map helps you develop a personalized toolkit of coping strategies for dealing with anxiety, providing a visual reference for implementing effective techniques during moments of heightened anxiety by:

- Creating a clear, easily accessible resource for a diverse range of effective anxiety management techniques.

- Recognizing patterns and connections between different coping methods.

- Developing a proactive, empowered approach to managing anxiety symptoms.

- Cultivating a sense of self-efficacy and resilience in the face of anxiety.

Instructions

1. Draw a central point representing your anxiety coping strategies. Label this "My Anxiety Coping Strategies."

2. Draw main branches from your central point for different categories of coping strategies, including

A. Relaxation techniques

B. Cognitive strategies

C. Lifestyle modifications

D. Social support and connection

E. Professional help and resources

3. Draw connecting lines between coping strategies that work well together or support one another.

4. Include a branch for noting any obstacles or challenges you may face in implementing certain coping strategies, like time constraints or lack of privacy, and brainstorm potential solutions or modifications.

5. Create a branch for tracking your progress and celebrating successes in using these coping strategies to manage anxiety.

Mind Mapping Exercises for ADHD Oppositional Defiance

Exercise 42: Mind Map Your Triggers for Oppositional Behavior

Objective

This mind map helps increase awareness of the factors that contribute to oppositional behavior by:

- Gaining insight into the underlying causes and patterns of oppositional behavior.

- Recognizing the emotional, environmental, and interpersonal factors that influence defiance.

- Identifying opportunities for proactive intervention and trigger management.

- Developing greater self-awareness and self-compassion in navigating oppositional tendencies.

Instructions

1. Draw a central point representing your triggers for oppositional behavior. Label this "My Oppositional Behavior Triggers."

2. Draw main branches from your central point for different categories of oppositional triggers, including

    A. Emotional triggers

    B. Environmental triggers

    C. Interpersonal triggers

    D. Physiological triggers

    E. Task-related triggers

3. Under each main branch, add twigs for specific examples or instances of these triggers in your own life.

4. Draw connecting lines between triggers that often occur together or seem to build on each other, indicating patterns or cycles of oppositional behavior.

5. Include a branch for the thoughts, feelings, or physical sensations that typically accompany each trigger.

6. Create a branch for proactive strategies or coping mechanisms that can help you manage or avoid specific triggers. You can source these from your previous exercises.

7. Review your oppositional behavior triggers mind map regularly, using it as a tool for self-awareness and proactive problem-solving.

Exercise 43: Mind Map Your Assertive Communication Strategies

Objective

This mind map aims to develop a mental step-by-step guide for assertively communicating needs and actively listening with the intent to understand instructions by:

- Clarifying your personal communication goals and values.

- Identifying the key components of assertive communication, such as "I" statements and active listening.

- Developing a structured approach to expressing your needs and perspectives respectfully.

- Practicing empathy and understanding when receiving feedback or instructions.

Instructions

1. Draw a central point representing your assertive communication strategies. Label this "My Assertive Communication Strategies."

2. Draw main branches from your central point for the key components of assertive communication, including

A. Expressing needs and boundaries clearly and directly

B. Using "I" statements to take ownership of your perspectives

C. Actively listening and seeking to understand others' viewpoints

D. Maintaining a calm, respectful tone and body language

E. Focusing on solutions and compromise rather than blame or defensiveness

3. Under each main branch, add twigs with specific strategies, phrases, or examples of how to implement these assertive communication techniques in real-life situations.

4. Include a branch for communication challenges or barriers you may face, including difficulty regulating emotions, fear of confrontation, or tendency to avoid conflict.

5. Brainstorm strategies for overcoming these obstacles.

6. Create a separate branch for practicing active listening skills, like giving your full attention and minimizing distractions.

7. Add a branch for self-care and emotional regulation strategies that can help you stay grounded and focused during challenging conversations.

8. Review your assertive communication mind map regularly, using it as a guide and reminder of the strategies and mindsets you want to cultivate in your interactions.

Exercise 44: Mind Map Your Positive Reinforcement Techniques for Cooperation

Objective

This mind map helps you create a visual reference of positive reinforcement strategies to reinforce desired behaviors and encourage cooperation by:

- Developing a proactive, strengths-based approach to behavior management.

- Identifying a variety of positive reinforcement methods to suit different situations and preferences.

- Recognizing the connection between specific behaviors and appropriate rewards or praise.

- Developing a more positive, encouraging atmosphere that promotes growth and cooperation.

Instructions

1. Draw a central point representing your positive reinforcement strategies. Label this "My Positive Reinforcement Strategies."

2. Draw main branches from your central point for different categories of positive reinforcement, including

    A. Verbal praise and acknowledgment

    B. Tangible rewards and privileges

    C. Quality time and shared activities

    D. Responsibility and trust-building opportunities

    E. Natural and logical consequences

3. Use colors, symbols, or images to represent the emotional impact or significance of different reinforcement strategies.

4. Draw connecting lines between reinforcement strategies that complement or build on each other.

5. Include a branch for noting the specific behaviors or achievements you want to reinforce. Link these behaviors to the relevant reinforcement strategies.

6. Create a branch for tracking the effectiveness of your reinforcement strategies and note any adjustments or modifications needed to maintain their impact over time.

7. Review your positive reinforcement mind map regularly, using it as a guide and inspiration for implementing consistent, affirming feedback and rewards.

Mind Mapping for ADHD Anger Management

Exercise 45: Mind Map Your Anger Triggers

Objective

This mind map helps you increase your awareness of specific triggers that contribute to anger episodes, allowing for better recognition and management of anger-provoking situations by:

- Gaining insight into the underlying causes and patterns of your anger responses.

- Recognizing the emotional, cognitive, and environmental factors that influence your anger.

- Identifying opportunities for proactive intervention and trigger management.

- Developing greater self-awareness and self-compassion in navigating anger-provoking situations.

Instructions

1. Draw a central point representing your anger triggers. Label this "My Anger Triggers."

2. Draw main branches from your central point for different categories of anger triggers, including

    A. Emotional triggers

    B. Cognitive triggers

    C. Environmental triggers

    D. Interpersonal triggers

    E. Physiological triggers

3. Under each main branch, add twigs for specific examples or instances of these triggers in your own life.

4. Draw connecting lines between triggers that often occur together or seem to build on each other, indicating patterns or cycles of anger responses.

5. Include a branch for the thoughts, feelings, or physical sensations that typically accompany each trigger, such as feeling powerless.

6. Create a branch for proactive strategies or coping mechanisms that can help you manage or prevent specific triggers.

7. Review your anger triggers mind map regularly, using it as a tool for self-awareness and proactive anger management.

Exercise 46: Mind Map Your Anger Expression Techniques

Objective

This mind map helps you develop a repertoire of healthy ways to express and manage anger, facilitating more effective communication and reducing the intensity and duration of anger episodes by:

- Identifying a range of appropriate and effective methods for communicating anger.

- Recognizing the importance of assertive communication, problem-solving, and emotional regulation in managing anger.

- Developing a structured approach to expressing anger in a controlled, respectful manner.

- Practicing techniques for de-escalating conflicts and maintaining composure during challenging situations.

Instructions

1. Draw a central point representing your anger expression techniques. Label this "My Anger Expression Techniques."

2. Draw main branches from your central point for different categories of anger expression techniques, including

A. Assertive communication

B. Problem-solving strategies

C. Emotional regulation techniques

3. Under each main branch, add twigs for specific techniques or strategies within that category.

4. Draw connecting lines between anger expression techniques that work well together or build on each other.

5. Include a branch for potential challenges or barriers to implementing these techniques, like difficulty regulating emotions in the heat of the moment.

6. Create a separate branch for tracking your progress and celebrating success when using these anger expression techniques effectively.

7. Review your anger expression mind map regularly, using it as a guide and reminder of the techniques and strategies you want to employ when faced with anger-provoking situations.

Exercise 47: Mind Map Your Calming Strategies for Anger

Objective

This mind map helps you compile a comprehensive list of calming strategies tailored to your preferences and needs, providing a visual reference for implementing effective techniques during moments of heightened anger. You will be:

- Identifying a diverse range of calming techniques and developing a personalized toolkit to draw upon in anger-provoking situations.

- Recognizing the importance of physical, mental, and sensory-based strategies in managing anger.

- Creating a clear, easily accessible guide for implementing calming strategies consistently and effectively.

- Cultivating a more balanced, resilient approach to managing intense emotions and stressors.

Instructions

1. Draw a central point representing your calming strategies for anger. Label this "My Calming Strategies for Anger."

2. Draw main branches from your central point for different categories of calming strategies, including

> A. Physical techniques

> B. Mental techniques

> C. Sensory-based techniques

3. Use colors, symbols, or images to represent the emotional impact or effectiveness of different calming strategies.

4. Draw connecting lines between calming strategies that complement or enhance each other.

5. Include a branch for noting any challenges or obstacles you may face when implementing certain calming strategies.

6.Brainstorm potential solutions or modifications.

7. Create a branch for tracking your progress and celebrating success when using these calming strategies to manage anger effectively.

8. Review your calming strategies mind map regularly, using it as a visual reminder and guide for implementing effective techniques during moments of heightened anger or frustration.

Mind Mapping for Learning New Tasks

Exercise 48: Mind Map Your Learning Objectives

Objective

This mind map helps you clarify your learning objectives and priorities. By identifying the specific learning objectives or goals you want to achieve, you will be:

• Gaining clarity on the purpose and desired outcomes of your learning.

• Prioritizing your learning objectives based on importance, relevance, or sequence, and identifying key knowledge areas, skills, or competencies to focus on.

• Creating a visual framework for organizing and structuring your learning path.

• Establishing a clear sense of direction and motivation for your learning efforts.

Instructions

1. Draw a central point representing your overall learning goal or topic. Label this with the name of the task or skill you want to learn.

2. Draw main branches from your central point for different categories or subtopics of learning objectives related to your main goal, including

    A. Fundamental concepts or principles

    B. Practical skills or techniques

    C. Relevant tools or technologies

    D. Industry standards or best practices

    E. Communication or collaboration skills

3. Under each main branch, add twigs for specific learning objectives within that category.

4. Draw connecting lines between learning objectives that are related, interdependent, or built upon each other.

5. Include a branch for resources, materials, or sources of information that can support your learning objectives.

6. Create a separate branch for timeline or milestone markers, breaking

down your learning journey into specific phases, deadlines, or checkpoints.

7. Review your learning objectives mind map regularly, using it as a guide and reference for focusing your learning objectives.

Exercise 49: Mind Map Your Step-By-Step Process for Learning

Objective

This mind map helps you develop a structured and systematic approach to learning so that it becomes easier to understand the necessary steps and actions involved in mastering the new task or skill by:

- Gaining a comprehensive overview of the learning process from start to finish.

- Identifying the key stages or milestones involved in developing mastery and the specific actions, practices, or strategies required at each step.

- Anticipating potential challenges or obstacles and planning how to overcome them.

- Creating a clear roadmap for progressing through the learning journey systematically.

Instructions

1. Draw a central point representing the overall learning process for your chosen task or skill. Label this "Learning Process for (Skill)."

2. Draw main branches from your central point for the key stages or phases of the learning process, including

A. Orientation or introduction to the topic

B. Foundational knowledge acquisition

C. Practical skill development and application

D. Refinement and advanced techniques

E. Integration and mastery

3. Under each main branch, add twigs for specific steps, actions, or strategies involved in that stage of the learning process, for example, completing structured lessons or tutorials or practicing key skills through exercises or drills.

4. Draw connecting lines between steps that are directly related or dependent on each other.

5. Include a branch for potential challenges, obstacles, or common mistakes that may arise at different stages of the learning process.

6. Note strategies or resources for overcoming these hurdles.

7. Create a separate branch for tracking your progress through the learning process, with checkboxes, progress bars, or other visual markers to indicate completed steps and milestones achieved.

8. Review your step-by-step learning process mind map regularly, using it as a guide and checklist for progressing through your learning journey systematically and efficiently.

Comorbid conditions are, unfortunately, very common for men with ADHD. However, by creating and using the aforementioned mind maps, you can develop a more intentional, structured, and effective approach to managing your comorbid conditions.

Chapter 9

Enhancing Motivation and Self-Discipline

Maintaining motivation and self-discipline can be an ongoing struggle with ADHD. It's not that we don't have a desire to achieve our goals and make positive changes. However, we find ourselves grappling with a lack of motivation, leading to difficulties with task initiation, persistence, and goal attainment. This inconsistency in motivation can be frustrating and demoralizing and may lead to a sense of self-doubt and inadequacy.

At the heart of this challenge lies the complex relationship between ADHD and the brain's reward system. Men with ADHD may have an underactive reward center, particularly in the dopamine-rich regions of the brain responsible for motivation, reinforcement, and goal-directed behavior. This neurological difference can make it difficult for us to experience the same sense of satisfaction and pleasure from completing tasks or achieving goals as our neurotypical peers.

These differences can mean our motivation deficits may manifest in different ways. Some of us may struggle with task initiation, finding it difficult to get started on projects or responsibilities, even when we intellectually know we need to. Others may start strong but battle with persistence, losing steam, or getting sidetracked before completing a task. Others may find it challenging to break down larger goals into manageable steps, leading to a sense of overwhelm and procrastination.

How ADHD Affects Motivation and Self-Discipline

To effectively address the challenges of motivation and self-discipline in adult men with ADHD, it's crucial to understand the underlying neurobiological and cognitive factors at play.

- At the core of motivation deficits in ADHD is a dysregulation of dopamine pathways in the brain. Dopamine is a neurotransmitter that plays a significant role in reward processing, reinforcement learning, and goal-directed behavior. In individuals with ADHD, there may be underactivity or an imbalance of dopamine in key brain regions, particularly in the mesolimbic and mesocortical pathways.

- Closely related to dopamine dysregulation is the concept of impaired reward processing in ADHD. As we now know, people with ADHD may have a blunted response to rewards, particularly when those rewards are delayed or require a sustained effort to achieve.

- Motivation and self-discipline are closely tied to executive functions: the higher-order cognitive processes that enable goal-directed behavior, impulse control, and self-regulation. In ADHD, there may be deficits in key executive function domains, including working memory, cognitive flexibility, and inhibitory control. These deficits can make it difficult to keep goals in mind, switch between tasks, and resist distractions, all essential for maintaining motivation and self-discipline.

- Another manifestation of dopamine dysregulation and impaired reward processing in ADHD is a tendency toward impulsivity and risk-taking behavior. Men with ADHD may have a harder time delaying gratification and considering the long-term consequences of their actions. This can lead to a preference for immediate, albeit smaller, rewards over larger, delayed ones.

It's important to note that these neurobiological and cognitive factors are not character flaws or personal failings but rather the result of the unique wiring of the ADHD brain.

The Role of Mind Mapping in Building Motivation and Self-Discipline

Mind mapping is a powerful tool to enhance motivation, improve self-discipline, and achieve goals. There are a number of ways mind mapping can help build motivation and self-discipline, including:

- It is easier to clearly define and visualize goals when creating a central point that represents a specific goal and then branching out to explore the various steps, milestones, and resources needed to achieve that goal.

- Mind mapping can also be valuable for developing actionable plans and tracking progress toward goals. Breaking down goals into specific tasks and subtasks and arranging them in a logical, sequential order allows us to create a clear roadmap for action.

- Another key aspect of building motivation and self-discipline is tapping into intrinsic motivators. These internal drivers and values give meaning and purpose to our goals.

- External rewards can be a powerful tool for building motivation and self-discipline, particularly when they are delivered frequently and consistently. Mind mapping can be used to create personalized reward systems that are tailored to individual preferences and goals.

- Finally, mind mapping can also be a valuable tool for identifying and developing strategies for overcoming barriers to self-discipline. Visually mapping out the specific challenges or obstacles that may arise in the pursuit of a goal can help us proactively brainstorm solutions and coping strategies.

Mind Mapping Exercises for Sustained Motivation

Exercise 50: Mind Map Your Loss of Motivation Triggers

Objective

This mind map helps you clarify your thought process to map your time better. It ensures tasks that cause a loss of motivation are done when energy levels and motivation are high by:

- Identifying specific tasks, situations, or factors that drain your motivation.

- Recognizing patterns or themes in your motivation struggles.

- Gaining insight into the underlying causes of your motivation challenges.

- Developing a proactive approach to managing your time and energy.

Instructions

1. Draw a central point representing your triggers for loss of motivation. Label this "My Loss of Motivation Triggers."

2. Draw main branches from your central point for different categories of motivation triggers, including

A. Task-related triggers

B. Emotional triggers

C. Environmental triggers

D. Physical triggers

E. Cognitive triggers

3. Under each main branch, draw twigs for specific examples or instances of these triggers in your own life. For example, "Complex, multi-step tasks."

4. Draw connecting lines between triggers that often occur together or seem to compound each other's effects, indicating patterns or cycles of motivation loss.

5. Include a branch for the thoughts, feelings, or behaviors that typically accompany each trigger.

6. Create a branch for proactive strategies or coping mechanisms that can help you manage or prevent specific motivation triggers. For example, "Breaking tasks into smaller steps."

7. Review your loss of motivation triggers mind map regularly, using it as a tool for self-awareness and proactive planning.

Exercise 51: Mind Map Your Personal Values and Motivators

Objective

This mind map helps you connect your intrinsic motivations and values, reinforcing their importance in guiding your actions and sustaining your motivation even during challenging times. You will be:

- Clarifying what matters most to you and why, recognizing the deeper purpose and meaning behind your goals and aspirations.

- Developing a stronger sense of intrinsic motivation and drive.

- Creating a framework for making decisions and prioritizing tasks aligned with your values.

- Cultivating a sense of authenticity and integrity in your actions.

Instructions

1. Draw a central point representing your personal values and motivators. Label this "My Personal Values and Motivators."

2. Draw main branches from your central point for different categories of values or motivators, including

   A. Ethical values

   B. Personal growth values

   C. Relationship values

   D. Professional values

   E. Lifestyle values

3. Under each main branch, add twigs for specific values, beliefs, or motivations within that category.

4. Draw connecting lines between values or motivators that are closely related or mutually reinforcing, indicating a web of interconnected drivers and aspirations.

5. Include a branch for specific goals, projects, or actions that align with and express each value or motivator.

6. Create a separate branch for potential conflicts or tensions between values, and brainstorm ways to navigate or reconcile these conflicts in your decision-making and goal-setting.

7. Review your personal values and motivators mind map regularly, using it as a guide and reminder of what matters most to you and why.

Exercise 52: Mind Map Your Progress Tracker and Rewards System

Objective

This mind map helps you establish a tangible way to monitor your progress and celebrate your successes, enhancing motivation and reinforcing positive behaviors. Develop a system for tracking your progress toward your goals and rewarding yourself for achievements by:

- Creating a clear, visual representation of your goals and milestones.

- Breaking down larger goals into specific, measurable steps or achievements.

- Developing a consistent, organized approach to monitoring your progress.

- Identifying meaningful rewards or incentives to celebrate your successes.

Instructions

1. Draw a central point representing your progress tracker and rewards system. Label this "My Progress Tracker and Rewards System."

2. Draw main branches from your central point for each of your major goals or areas of focus, including

A. Professional development goals

B. Health and fitness goals

C. Creative or personal project goals

D. Financial or savings goals

E. Relationship or social connection goals

3. Under each main branch, draw twigs for specific milestones or achievements that represent progress toward that goal.

4. Draw connecting lines between milestones that build on each other or represent a logical sequence of progress.

5. Use colors, symbols, or images to indicate each milestone's level of effort or significance.

6. Include a branch for the specific metrics, tools, or systems you will use to track your progress.

7. Create a separate branch for the rewards or incentives you will use to celebrate your achievements, with specific rewards matched to different levels or types of milestones.

8. Add a branch for reflecting on your progress and adjusting your goals or strategies as needed, with prompts for regular check-ins and self-assessment.

Exercise 53: Mind Map Your Visualization of Success

Objective

This mind map helps you harness the power of visualization to inspire and motivate yourself, reinforcing your commitment to achieving your goals and aspirations by:

- Clarifying your personal vision of success, creating a vivid, compelling mental image of your desired outcomes.

- Engaging your imagination and emotions in the pursuit of your goals.

- Reinforcing your belief in your ability to achieve your aspirations.

- Tapping into the motivational power of positive anticipation and expectancy.

Instructions

1. Draw a central point representing your visualization of success. Label this "My Visualization of Success."

2. Draw main branches from your central point for different aspects or dimensions of your success vision, including

A. Professional or career success

B. Personal growth and development

C. Relationships and social connections

D. Health and well-being

E. Financial abundance and security

F. Lifestyle and experiences

3. Under each main branch, add twigs for specific words, images, scenes, or symbols that represent your vision of success.

4. Use colors, textures, and visual details to make your visualization as vivid and engaging as possible.

5. Draw connecting lines between different aspects of your vision of success that are interrelated or mutually supportive.

6. Create a separate branch for affirmations, mantras, or quotes that encapsulate the essence of your success vision and reinforce your belief in its attainment.

7. Add a branch for specific actions, habits, or milestones that will move you closer to your vision of success.

8. Review your visualization of success mind map regularly. Immerse yourself in the mental experience of your desired outcomes, and let the positive emotions and expectations fuel your motivation and drive.

Exercise 54: Mind Map Your Daily Avoidance Tasks to Increase Self-Discipline

Objective

This mind map helps you establish a structured routine where your loss of motivation habits are included in motivation routines. You will be:

• Identifying the specific tasks or activities that you typically avoid or procrastinate on.

• Developing a systematic approach to integrating avoidance tasks into your daily routine.

• Creating a clear, visual plan for building self-discipline and overcoming challenges with motivation.

• Harnessing the power of habit stacking and environmental cues to make avoidance tasks more automatic and effortless.

Instructions

1. Draw a central point representing your daily avoidance tasks. Label this "My Daily Avoidance Tasks."

2. Draw main branches from your central point for different categories of avoidance tasks, such as

A. Household chores and maintenance

B. Administrative or paperwork tasks

C. Health and self-care routines

D. Skill-building or learning activities

F. Interpersonal or communication tasks

3. Under each main branch, add twigs for specific avoidance tasks within the category that you identified in previous exercises.

4. For each specific avoidance task, create a new twig for an existing routine, habit, or environmental cue that you can link that task to.

5. Draw connecting lines between avoidance tasks that can be grouped or completed sequentially, creating a flow or momentum of self-disciplined action throughout your day.

6. Include a branch for specific rewards, treats, or self-acknowledg-

ments you will give yourself for consistently completing your daily avoidance tasks.

7. Create a separate branch for tracking your completion of daily avoidance tasks, like checkboxes or progress bars.

8. Review your daily avoidance tasks mind map each morning and evening, using it as a guide and accountability tool for building self-discipline and overcoming procrastination.

Exercise 55: Mind Map Your Accountability Behaviors

Objective

This mind map helps you cultivate self-accountability behaviors to self-motivate and develop self-discipline by:

- Recognizing the importance of personal responsibility and ownership in your self-discipline journey.

- Identifying specific actions, habits, or routines that can serve as accountability anchors.

- Developing a proactive, self-directed approach to monitoring and regulating your behavior.

- Creating a clear, visual framework for integrating accountability into your daily life.

Instructions

1. Draw a central point representing your accountability behaviors. Label this "My Accountability Behaviors."

2. Draw main branches from your central point for different areas of your life where you want to develop self-accountability, including

    A. Personal health and well-being

    B. Work or career development

    C. Relationships and communication

    D. Financial management and decision-making

    E. Learning and skill acquisition

3. Under each main branch, add twigs for specific behaviors, habits, or routines that can serve as accountability triggers or reinforcers in that area. For example, you could log your food intake or exercise sessions or set clear goals and deadlines for work projects.

4. Draw connecting lines between accountability behaviors that are related or mutually reinforcing.

5. Include a branch for specific tools, systems, or resources to support your accountability behaviors, such as apps, calendars, or progress trackers.

6. Create a separate branch for rewards, celebrations, or self-acknowledgments you will give yourself for consistently demonstrating accountability and making progress.

7. Review your accountability behaviors mind map regularly, using it as a guide and reminder of the specific actions and habits that will keep you on track and motivated.

Exercise 56: Mind Map Your Self-Discipline Strategies and Techniques

Objective

This mind map helps you develop a toolkit of self-discipline strategies and techniques to overcome procrastination, distractions, and temptations, developing greater consistency and focus in pursuing your goals by:

- Identifying a range of proven, effective approaches to building self-discipline.

- Developing a systematic, organized framework for implementing self-discipline techniques that work for you.

- Creating a clear, accessible reference guide for overcoming motivation and willpower challenges.

- Cultivating a growth mindset and openness to experimenting with new self-discipline methods.

Instructions

1. Draw a central point representing your self-discipline strategies and techniques. Label this "My Self-Discipline Strategies and Techniques."

2. Draw main branches from your central point for different categories of self-discipline strategies, including

    A. Goal-setting and planning techniques

    B. Time management and scheduling methods

    C. Motivation and rewards systems

    D. Habit formation and tracking strategies

    E. Mindset and perspective-shifting techniques

3. Under each main branch, add twigs for specific strategies, techniques, or tools within that category, e.g., SMART goal-setting framework or habit stacking for building new routines.

4. Draw connecting lines between strategies that complement or enhance each other.

5. Include a branch for potential obstacles, challenges, or resistance you may face in implementing certain self-discipline strategies, and brainstorm ways to overcome these barriers.

6. Create a separate branch for tracking your experimentation and progress with different self-discipline techniques.

7. Review your self-discipline strategies and techniques mind map regularly, using it as a source of inspiration, guidance, and support in your ongoing self-discipline practice.

Exercise 57: Mind Map Your Reflection and Evaluation Process

Objective

This mind map helps develop self-awareness and continuous improvement by regularly reflecting on your actions, behaviors, and progress, thus refining your self-discipline and goal-setting strategies over time. You will be:

- Recognizing the importance of self-reflection and feedback in the self-discipline journey.

- Developing a visual, structured, intentional approach to assessing your progress and identifying growth opportunities.

- Identifying key questions, prompts, and criteria for meaningful self-assessment.

- Cultivating a growth mindset and openness to learning from both successes and challenges.

Instructions

1. Draw a central point representing your reflection and evaluation process. Label this "My Reflection and Evaluation Process."

2. Draw main branches from your central point for different aspects or dimensions of your self-discipline and goal pursuit that you want to reflect on and evaluate regularly, including

A. Progress toward specific goals or milestones

B. Effectiveness of current strategies, techniques, and habits

C. Challenges, obstacles, or setbacks encountered

    D. Insights, learnings, or growth opportunities identified

    E. Alignment with values, priorities, and long-term vision

3. Under each main branch, add twigs for specific questions, prompts, or criteria you will use to guide your reflection and evaluation in that area. For example, "What progress have I made toward my goal this week–month?" Or, "Which strategies or techniques have been most effective in supporting my self-discipline?"

4. Draw connecting lines between different aspects of your reflection and evaluation that are interrelated or mutually informing.

5. Include a branch for action steps, adjustments, or experiments you want to implement based on your reflections and evaluations.

6. Create a separate branch for celebrating your progress, successes, and learning as a way to maintain motivation.

7. Review your reflection and evaluation mind map regularly, using it as a guide and prompt for your ongoing self-assessment practice.

Exercise 58: Mind Map Your Growth Mindset and Resilience Techniques

Objective

This mind map helps you develop a mindset of resilience and adaptability, empowering yourself to persevere in the face of obstacles and setbacks, thus strengthening your self-discipline and determination by:

- Becoming more flexible and creating an adaptive approach to navigating adversity and change.

- Recognizing the value of challenges and setbacks as opportunities for learning and growth.

- Identifying specific strategies, affirmations, and practices for cultivating resilience.

• Creating a clear, accessible reference guide for maintaining a growth mindset in the face of difficulty.

Instructions

1. Draw a central point representing your growth mindset and resilience techniques. Label this "My Growth Mindset and Resilience Techniques."

2. Draw main branches from your central point for different aspects or principles of a growth mindset, including

    A. Embracing challenges as opportunities for growth

    B. Learning from failures and setbacks

    C. Focusing on effort and progress over perfection

    D. Cultivating a love of learning and curiosity

    E. Seeking feedback and constructive criticism

    D. Celebrating the journey of development and improvement

3. Under each main branch, draw twigs for specific techniques, strategies, or practices that support that aspect of a growth mindset. These could include reframing negative self-talk and limiting beliefs, or practicing self-compassion and kindness in the face of setbacks.

4. Draw connecting lines between principles and techniques that are related or mutually reinforcing.

5. Include a branch for affirmations, quotes, or mantras that encapsulate the essence of a growth mindset and resilience.

6. Create a separate branch for real-life examples, role models, or success stories that demonstrate the power of a growth mindset and resilience in overcoming obstacles and achieving goals.

7. Review your growth mindset and resilience techniques mind map regularly, using it as a source of inspiration, encouragement, and guidance in the face of challenges or setbacks.

Building and sustaining motivation and self-discipline is a lifelong journey of personal growth and development. While it is true that motivation can be fleeting, it is possible, even for neurodivergent individuals, to cultivate a more consistent, reliable sense of drive and determination through intentional practice and self-reflection.

Chapter 10

Creating Healthy Habits for ADHD Symptom Management

The great thing in the world is not so much where we stand as in what direction we are moving.

Oiver Wendell Holmes

For adult men with ADHD, creating and maintaining healthy habits can be a significant challenge. The very nature of ADHD, with its difficulties in executive functioning, impulsivity, and consistency, can make it tough to establish and stick to routines that promote physical, emotional, and mental well-being. However, understanding the science of habit formation and leveraging the power of mind mapping can be a game-changer in overcoming these challenges and building sustainable, healthy habits.

The Impact of ADHD on Habit Formation

A habit is a behavior that has been repeated enough times to become automatic. Whether it's brushing your teeth in the morning, checking your phones, or reaching for a snack when you're stressed, your habits shape your daily lives and, over time, your health and well-being. Habits are neither good nor bad, but all of them can be broken down into three key components: trigger, action, and reward.

The trigger is the cue or prompt that initiates the habitual behavior. It can be internal, like feelings of boredom or stress, or external, like a notification on your phone. When you encounter the trigger, it sets off an automatic response or action, which is the behavior itself. This could be scrolling through social media or going for a run. Finally, there is the reward, which is the positive reinforcement that your brain

"

associates with the behavior. This could be a temporary relief of stress, the dopamine hit from social media likes, or the endorphin rush after exercise.

For men with ADHD, the challenges in habit formation often lie in the interplay between these three components. Due to differences in the brain's reward system and difficulties with impulse control, individuals with ADHD may be more susceptible to triggers that promote unhealthy habits, such as procrastination or substance use. The actions themselves may be more challenging to initiate or sustain due to issues with task initiation, follow-through, and consistency. And the rewards may feel less satisfying or motivating, making it harder to reinforce the positive behavior over time.

Mind Mapping for Creating Healthy Habits

Mind mapping is a powerful tool for creating healthy habits. Visually mapping out our current habits and patterns allows us to identify opportunities to stack new, healthy behaviors onto established ones. This can make the process of habit formation more manageable and automatic. Mind mapping offers a structured approach to habit formation by:

- Identifying existing rituals and routines that can serve as a foundation for new habits, such as brushing our teeth, taking lunch breaks, or watching TV in the evening.

- Visually mapping out the details of our daily routines, making it easier to spot opportunities for adding new, healthy habits.

- Creating specific implementation intentions for when, where, and how we will perform new habits, making them feel more concrete and actionable.

- Using habit stacking to piggyback new behaviors onto existing ones.

- Tracking our progress and celebrating successes by adding

visual markers or checkmarks to our mind map as we complete new habits.

Leveraging the power of habit stacking and implementing intentions using mind mapping can help us visually plan and track our progress toward building healthy habits.

Mind Mapping Exercises for Building Healthy Habits

Exercise 59: Mind Map Your Morning Waking Rituals

Objective

This exercise aims to visually map out your morning waking routine, allowing you to gain insights into your habitual behaviors and identify opportunities for enhancement. You will be:

- Gaining insights into your habitual behaviors and identifying opportunities for enhancement.

- Cultivating mindfulness and intentionality in your morning rituals.

- Optimizing your routine for productivity and well-being.

- Setting a positive tone for the rest of your day.

Instructions

1. Draw a central point representing your morning routine. Label this "My Morning Routine."

2. Draw main branches from your central point for different stages of your morning routine, including

A. Waking up and getting out of bed

B. Personal hygiene and grooming

C. Breakfast and nutrition

D. Physical activity or exercise

E. Mental preparation and planning

D. Commuting or transitioning to work

3. Under each main branch, add twigs for specific actions, habits, or rituals within that stage of your morning routine, e.g., brushing your teeth, showering, or getting dressed.

4. Draw connecting lines between areas of your morning routine that are related or influence each other, such as the link between waking up late and skipping breakfast or the connection between physical activity and mental clarity.

5. Draw twigs for the approximate duration of each stage or component of your morning routine.

6. Create a separate branch for noting any inconsistencies, challenges, or pain points in your current morning routine.

Exercise 60: Mind Map Your Morning Routine Enhancement

Objective

This mind map enhances your morning routine by integrating healthy habits that promote productivity, focus, and well-being. You will be:

- Recognizing the impact of your morning habits on your overall well-being and performance.

- Identifying specific areas for growth and improvement in your morning routine.

- Exploring new habits, rituals, or practices that align with your goals and values.

• Creating a clear, inspiring vision of your optimal morning experience.

Instructions

1. Draw a central point representing your enhanced morning routine. Label this "My Ideal Morning Routine."

2. Draw main branches from your central point for different themes of your ideal morning routine, such as

  A. Mindfulness and mental clarity

  B. Physical vitality and energy

  C. Nourishment and hydration

  D. Productivity and focus

  E. Connection and gratitude

  F. Self-care and personal growth

3. Under each main branch, add twigs for specific habits, rituals, or practices you want to incorporate. These could include meditation, deep breathing, journaling, or a nutritious breakfast (e.g., smoothie or herbal tea).

4. Draw connecting lines between components of your ideal morning routine that support or enhance each other.

5. Draw twigs for the estimated time allocation or duration of each stage of your ideal morning routine.

6. Create a separate branch for the specific action steps, resources, or support you may need to implement your ideal morning routine.

7. Review your morning routine enhancement mind map regularly, using it as a source of guidance and motivation as you work toward transforming your mornings.

Exercise 61: Mind Map Your Physical Activity Plan

Objective

This mind map helps you establish a personalized physical activity plan that fits your preferences and lifestyle, facilitating a habit of regular exercise for improved health and symptom management. You will be:

- Identifying the types of physical activity that align with your interests and abilities.

- Exploring ways to integrate more movement and exercise into your daily life.

- Developing a balanced, sustainable approach to consistent exercise and physical fitness.

- Cultivating a sense of commitment and motivation toward your physical well-being.

Instructions

1. Draw a central point representing your physical activity plan. Label this "My Physical Activity Plan."

2. Draw main branches from your central point for different categories or settings for physical activity, including

   A. Home-based workouts

   B. Outdoor activities

   C. Gym or fitness center

   D. Group classes or sports

3. Under each main branch, draw twigs for specific types of physical activity or exercises you enjoy or want to try.

4. Draw connecting lines between types of physical activity that complement or alternate with each other.

5. Draw twigs for the specific days, times, or triggers for engaging in each type of physical activity.

6. Create a separate branch for tracking your progress, celebrating your achievements, and adjusting your plan as needed.

7. Review your physical activity plan mind map regularly, using it as a guide and reminder of your commitment to an active, healthy lifestyle.

Exercise 62: Mind Map Your Meal-Planning Strategy

Objective

This mind map helps develop a structured meal-planning strategy that supports healthy eating habits and reduces impulsivity or reliance on convenience foods. You will be:

- Gaining awareness of your current eating patterns and their impact on your health and well-being, including identifying specific areas for improvement.

- Exploring healthy meal ideas and recipes that align with your preferences and nutritional needs.

- Creating a clear, organized plan for grocery shopping and meal preparation.

- Developing a routine or system for consistent, efficient meal planning and execution.

Instructions

1. Draw a central point representing your meal-planning strategy. Label this "My Meal-Planning Strategy."

2. Draw main branches from your central point for the different stages of your meal-planning process, including

A. Assessing current eating habits and areas for improvement

B. Researching and selecting healthy meal ideas and recipes

C. Creating grocery lists and shopping for ingredients

D. Preparing and cooking meals in advance

E. Storing and reheating pre-prepared meals

F. Evaluating and adjusting meal plans based on experience and preferences

3. Under each main branch, draw twigs for specific strategies, tools, or actions related to that stage of the meal-planning process. For example, you could keep a food diary or use a tracking app to monitor current eating patterns.

4. Draw connecting lines between areas of your meal-planning strategy that are related or mutually reinforcing.

5. Include a branch for potential obstacles or challenges you may face when implementing your meal-planning strategy.

6. Create a separate branch for tracking your progress, celebrating your successes, and making adjustments to your meal-planning strategy as needed.

Exercise 63: Mind Map Your Recreation Time

Objective

This mind map helps cultivate a life of balance by *not* depriving yourself of the things you want to do while still doing the things you need to do. You will be:

- Identifying activities that bring you joy, relaxation, and fulfillment.

- Recognizing the value of leisure time and self-care in maintaining overall well-being

• Creating a balanced, diversified approach to integrating your recreational interests into your routine.

• Establishing a healthy work-life balance that supports your mental and emotional health.

Instructions

1. Begin with a central point representing your recreation–hobby time. Label this "My Recreation Time."

2. Draw main branches from your central point for different categories or types of recreational activities and hobbies. For example

A. Outdoor adventures and nature-based activities

B. Creative pursuits and artistic expressions.

C. Social events and community involvement

D. Physical activities and sports

E. Intellectual pursuits and learning opportunities

F. Relaxation and self-care practices

3. Under each main branch, draw twigs for specific activities, interests, or hobbies you enjoy or want to explore.

4. Draw connecting lines between recreational activities or hobbies that complement or enhance each other.

5. Draw twigs for the specific benefits or positive outcomes you hope to gain from each recreational activity or hobby.

6. Create a separate branch for the resources needed to engage in each activity.

Exercise 64: Mind Map Your Winding Down Strategies

Objective

This mind map allows you to develop winding down strategies so that you have insights into the effectiveness of your current relaxation routine and identify opportunities for improvement. You will be:

- Gaining awareness of your current relaxation habits and their impact on your sleep quality.

- Identifying specific strategies or activities that promote relaxation and prepare you for restful sleep.

- Exploring new techniques or practices that may enhance your winding down routine.

- Creating a clear, personalized plan for optimizing your evening relaxation and sleep preparation.

Instructions

1. Draw a central point representing your winding down strategies. Label this "My Winding Down Strategies."

2. Draw main branches from your central point for different components or stages of your winding down routine, for example

A. Transitioning from work or daily activities to relaxation mode

B. Engaging in calming or stress-reducing activities. For example, hobbies, dance, or art

C. Preparing your sleep environment and bedtime rituals

D. Practicing relaxation techniques or mindfulness exercises

3. Under each main branch, draw twigs for specific strategies, activities, or practices related to that stage of the winding down process. For example, setting a designated end time for work or screen use.

4. Draw connecting lines between winding down strategies that are related or mutually supportive.

5. Draw a branch for potential obstacles or challenges you may face when implementing your winding down strategies.

6. Create a separate branch for tracking your progress, celebrating your successes, and making adjustments to your winding down routine as needed.

7. Review your winding down strategies mind map regularly, using it as a guide and reminder of your commitment to relaxation, sleep hygiene, and self-care. Update the map as you discover new techniques, refine your evening routines, or overcome obstacles to restful sleep.

Exercise 65: Mind Map Your Sleep Hygiene Routine

Objective

This mind map helps establish a consistent sleep hygiene routine that promotes restful sleep and enhances overall well-being and symptom management. You will be:

- Gaining awareness of your current sleep patterns and their impact on your health and well-being, including identifying specific habits or environmental factors that may be hindering your sleep quality.

- Exploring evidence-based practices and techniques for improving sleep hygiene.

- Creating a clear, personalized plan for optimizing your sleep environment and bedtime routines.

- Recognizing the critical role of healthy sleep in managing symptoms and promoting overall wellness.

Instructions

1. Draw a central point representing your sleep hygiene routine. Label this "My Sleep Hygiene Routine."

2. Draw main branches from your central point for different components or categories of sleep hygiene practices, including

   A. Sleep environment optimization

   B. Pre-bedtime rituals and routines

   C. Lifestyle factors affecting sleep

   D. Relaxation and stress-reduction techniques, such as sleep scheduling and consistency

   E. Sleep tracking and evaluation

3. Under each main branch, draw twigs for specific strategies, habits, or practices related to that category of sleep hygiene, e.g., limiting caffeine, alcohol, and heavy meals close to bedtime.

4. Draw connecting lines between sleep hygiene practices that are related or mutually reinforcing.

5. Create a separate branch for incorporating the winding down strategies from the previous exercise into your sleep hygiene routine.

6. Review your sleep hygiene mind map regularly, using it as a guide and reminder of your commitment to prioritizing and optimizing your sleep health.

Creating and using these mind maps can help you develop a comprehensive, personalized approach to habit stacking so that you can build great habits for your life. With great habits comes better symptom management, and ultimately, the more easily you manage your symptoms, the better your well-being will become.

Download your free bonus to learn more about apps that help with building new habits

https://selftransformationpath.com/BundlePB
You can also scan this QR code to get access.

Chapter 11
Improving ADHD Creativity

Men with ADHD possess a unique blend of traits that can fuel remarkable creativity. Their minds often buzz with a constant stream of ideas, associations, and possibilities, allowing them to make connections that others might miss. This divergent thinking style, combined with a tendency for spontaneity and an ability to hyperfocus on topics of interest, can lead to truly original and innovative ideas.

Creativity is different with ADHD because we process information differently. While neurotypical brains tend to follow linear, sequential thinking patterns, ADHD brains often jump from one idea to another, exploring various concepts and making unexpected connections. This nonlinear, associative thinking style can be a powerful asset if we know how to tap into it without becoming distracted.

The Manifestation of ADHD Creativity

ADHD creativity can manifest in different areas of our lives, including artistic expression and innovative problem-solving. Understanding how ADHD creativity can take shape in men with ADHD allows us to begin identifying and cultivating our unique creative strengths and passions.

In the workplace, male employees with ADHD can bring fresh perspectives, innovative ideas, and creative energy to their teams and organizations. They may be particularly skilled at identifying inefficiencies, generating alternative solutions, and adapting to changing market conditions. Fostering an inclusive culture that values neurodiversity and supports the unique strengths of male employees with ADHD allows organizations to tap into a powerful source of creativity and innovation.

However, it's important to recognize that ADHD creativity can also come with challenges and potential pitfalls. The same divergent thinking and impulsivity that fuel original ideas can also lead to distractibility, disorganization, and difficulty following through on projects. Furthermore, the emotional intensity and sensitivity that often accompany ADHD can make the creative process feel over-whelming or draining at times.

Mind Mapping for Enhancing ADHD Creativity

Mind mapping is a powerful tool for channeling and amplifying our creative potential. By providing a visual, nonlinear framework for brainstorming, organizing ideas, and exploring connections, mind mapping aligns naturally with the divergent thinking style and associative processing of the ADHD brain. Here are some key ways in which mind mapping can support and enhance ADHD creativity:

- Mind mapping is an incredibly effective tool for brainstorming and generating new ideas.

- While ADHD creativity can generate a wealth of original ideas, it can sometimes be challenging to organize and structure those ideas into a coherent whole.

- One of the unique strengths of ADHD creativity is the ability to make novel connections and associations between seemingly unrelated ideas or concepts.

- Creativity is rarely a one-and-done process. Mind mapping provides a flexible, dynamic framework for this iterative process, allowing for the easy addition, modification, or rearrangement of ideas as they develop.

Mind Mapping Exercises for Building Creativity

Exercise 66: Mind Map Your Creative Passions

Objective

This mind map identifies and nurtures your creative passions, creating a sense of fulfillment and purpose when pursuing your passions by:

- Gaining clarity on the creative activities and projects that inspire and energize you.

- Identifying patterns or themes in your creative interests and aspirations.

- Exploring new or untapped areas of creative potential and curiosity.

- Cultivating a mindset of creative exploration, growth, and self-expression.

Instructions

1. Draw a central point representing your creative passions. Label this "My Creative Passions."

2. Draw main branches from your central point for different categories of creative pursuits, including

A. Painting, drawing, or photography

B. Music, dance, or theater

C. Writing, poetry, or storytelling

D. Woodworking, knitting, or ceramics

E. Graphic design, video editing, animation

F. Cooking or baking

3. Under each main branch, draw twigs for specific creative activities, projects, or interests you currently engage in or would like to explore. For example, sketching and illustration or designing websites or mobile apps.

4. Draw connecting lines between creative pursuits that are related or could potentially intersect, such as photography and graphic design.

5. Include a branch for the skills, resources, or inspiration you may need to develop or explore each creative passion.

6. Create a separate branch for the potential outcomes, benefits, or personal growth you hope to achieve.

Exercise 67: Mind Map Your Creative Ideas

Objective

This mind map helps stimulate creative thinking and ideation by generating a pool of innovative ideas. You will be:

- Unleashing your creative potential and generating a diverse range of ideas and possibilities.

- Breaking free from habitual thinking patterns and cultivating a mindset of curiosity, openness, and creative experimentation.

- Identifying compelling themes, concepts, or questions to guide your creative projects.

- Developing a resource of inspiration and potential starting points for future creative work.

Instructions

1. Draw a central point representing your brainstorming session. Label it "Creative Project Ideas."

2. Draw main branches from your central point for different categories or themes of creative project ideas, such as

> A. Social impact and community engagement projects
>
> B. Personal growth and self-discovery projects
>
> C. Environmental and sustainability-focused projects
>
> D. Technology and innovation-driven projects
>
> E. Collaborative and interdisciplinary projects

3. Under each main branch, draw twigs for specific project ideas, concepts, or questions. For example, you might want to create a community art installation that promotes dialogue and understanding.

4. Draw connecting lines between project ideas that share similar themes, approaches, or potential synergies.

5. Include a branch for the resources, inspiration, or research you may need to develop each project idea further or refine it.

6. Update the map as you generate new ideas, refine existing concepts, or embark on new creative projects and collaborations.

Exercise 68: Mind Map Your Creative Problem-Solving Strategies

Objective

This mind map helps you cultivate a mindset of creative problem-solving, empowering you to overcome obstacles and navigate challenges with ingenuity and resourcefulness. You will accomplish:

- Gaining clarity on the nature and scope of the challenges or obstacles you are facing, and identifying patterns, connections, or insights that can guide your problem-solving efforts.

- Generating a diverse range of potential solutions, approaches, and perspectives.

- Developing a visual toolkit of creative strategies and resources for overcoming challenges.

- Cultivating a sense of agency, resilience, and creative confidence in the face of obstacles.

Instructions

1. Draw a central point representing the challenge or obstacle you are currently facing. Label this with a clear, concise description of the problem. For example, "Work presentation anxiety."

2. Draw main branches from your central point for different aspects or factors of the problem, including

    A. Technical or logistical challenges

    B. Financial or resource constraints

    C. Interpersonal or communication difficulties

    D. Conceptual or creative blocks

    E. Emotional or motivational barriers

    F. External or environmental factors

3. Under each main branch, draw twigs for specific details or examples, e.g., "Technical or logistical challenges = lack of access to necessary tools or equipment."

4. Draw connecting lines between aspects of the problem that are related, interconnected, or potentially mutually reinforcing, for example, between financial constraints and technical limitations.

5. Include a branch for generating potential solutions, strategies, or approaches for addressing each aspect of the problem, for example, researching alternative tools, materials, or production methods.

6. Create a separate branch for identifying resources, support systems, or mentors who can help you navigate and overcome the challenges.

Exercise 69: Mind Map Your Future Creative Endeavors

Objective

This mind map clarifies your creative vision and sets actionable goals, providing a roadmap for realizing your creative aspirations and bringing your ideas to fruition. You will be:

- Gaining clarity on your desired creative outcomes and achievements.

- Identifying the resources, skills, and support needed to realize your creative vision.

- Developing a sense of direction, purpose, and motivation in your creative pursuits.

- Cultivating a mindset of long-term planning, strategic thinking, and proactive goal-setting.

Instructions

1. Draw a central point representing your future creative endeavors. Label this "My Future Creative Endeavors."

2. Draw main branches from your central point for different categories or domains of your creative aspirations, including

A. Professional achievements and recognition

B. Personal growth and skill development

C. Collaborative partnerships and projects

D. Community impact and social change

E. Legacy and long-term influence

F. Creative experimentation and innovation

3. Under each main branch, draw twigs for specific goals, milestones, or achievements you hope to achieve, e.g., mastering a new creative technique or medium.

4. Draw connecting lines between future creative endeavors that are related to each other.

5. Include a branch for the specific action steps, habits, or practices you will need to implement to progress with each future creative endeavor, such as developing a consistent creative practice.

6. Create a separate branch for the potential challenges, obstacles, or risks you may face in pursuing your future creative endeavors, and brainstorm strategies or mindsets for overcoming these challenges.

7. Review your future creative endeavors mind map regularly, using it as a source of guidance and accountability.

Exercise 70: Mind Map Your Connections Between Ideas

Objective

This mind map helps creativity through associative thinking, uncovering new insights and possibilities by exploring the relationships between dissimilar ideas. You will be:

- Engaging in divergent thinking and generating a diverse range of ideas and associations.

- Identifying patterns, themes, or underlying principles that link seemingly unrelated concepts, therefore creating a visual web of interconnected ideas and potential creative directions.

- Developing a more holistic, integrative understanding of your creative domain or challenge.

- Cultivating a mindset of curiosity, open-mindedness, and creative exploration.

Instructions

1. Draw a central point representing the core idea, theme, or challenge you want to explore. Label this with a clear, concise description of the central concept. For example, "My thesis" or "Creative business launch ideas."

2. Draw main branches from your central point for different categories, aspects, or dimensions of the core idea, including

> A. Conceptual or theoretical foundations
>
> B. Historical or cultural contexts
>
> C. Aesthetic or formal qualities
>
> D. Emotional or psychological resonance
>
> E. Social or political implications
>
> F. Technological or material possibilities

3. Under each main branch, draw twigs for specific ideas or examples, such as "Conceptual or theoretical foundations = uncover limiting beliefs or thought frameworks."

4. Draw connecting lines between ideas or concepts that share similar themes or patterns.

5. Include a branch for writing down questions or contradictions that emerge from exploring the connections between ideas.

6. Create a separate branch for brainstorming potential applications, projects, or creative expressions that could emerge from the interconnected web of ideas.

Exercise 71: Mind Map Your Flow State Strategies

Objective

This mind map helps you visually map out the strategies and conditions that facilitate your flow state. It allows you to gain insights into how to cultivate optimal conditions for deep focus, creativity, and productivity by:

• Gaining clarity on the specific tasks or contexts that naturally evoke a flow state for you.

• Identifying the external and internal conditions that support your deep focus and engagement.

• Exploring the mindset, rituals, or techniques that help you enter and maintain a flow state.

• Developing a more intentional, proactive approach to cultivating flow in your creative practice through creating a visual guide or checklist for optimizing your environment and mindset.

Instructions

1. Draw a central point representing your flow state experiences. Label this "My Flow State Strategies."

2. Draw main branches from your central point for different categories of flow state facilitators, including

A. Activities or tasks that stimulate flow

B. Environmental factors or settings

C. Mindset or mental strategies

D. Rituals or preparatory techniques

E. Collaboration or social dynamics

F. Tools or resources

3. Under each main branch, draw twigs for specific examples, practices, or conditions that contribute to your flow state in that category. For example, these could be writing, coding, or designing for extended

periods without interruption or working in a quiet, clutter-free space with natural light and inspiring views.

4. Draw connecting lines between flow state strategies that work together or reinforce each other, like the link between a clutter-free environment and a focused mindset.

5. Include a branch for capturing any obstacles, distractions, or challenges that typically disrupt your flow state, and brainstorm strategies for minimizing or overcoming these barriers.

6. Create a separate branch for tracking your progress, insights, and achievements in implementing your flow state strategies, celebrating the moments of heightened creativity, productivity, and fulfillment.

Exercise 72: Mind Map Your Creative Inspirations

Objective

This mind map helps expand your creative horizons and draws inspiration from diverse sources, enriching your creative practice and fueling innovation. You will be:

- Identifying the artists, thinkers, experiences, and environments that spark your creativity and imagination.

- Exploring the common themes, qualities, or ideas that resonate across your diverse inspirations.

- Discovering new connections, patterns, or possibilities by analyzing alternative sources of inspiration.

- Creating a rich, dynamic tapestry of influences and references to inform and enrich your creative work.

Instructions

1. Draw a central point representing your creative inspirations. Label this "My Creative Inspirations."

2. Draw main branches from your central point for different categories of creative inspirations. For example

    A. Visual artists and designers

    B. Musicians and composers

    C. Writers and poets

    D. Filmmakers and actors

    E. Architects and urban planners

    F. Scientists and researchers

3. Under each main branch, add subbranches for specific examples, works, or aspects of your inspirations in that category, e.g., a song or album that stimulates you.

4. Draw connecting lines between inspirations that share common themes, qualities, or ideas, revealing the underlying patterns, tensions, or possibilities that animate your creative vision and practice.

5. Include a branch for capturing the key insights, questions, or creative sparks that you uncover from exploring your inspirations, and brainstorm potential ways to translate these insights.

6. Create a separate branch for identifying new sources of inspiration to seek out and engage with, like attending exhibitions, performances, or lectures, traveling to new destinations, or connecting with creative communities and collaborators.

Exercise 73: Mind Map Your Creative Collaboration Opportunities

Objective

This mind map helps you foster collaborative creativity and leverage the strengths and perspectives of others. You will be:

- Recognizing the value of collaboration and interdisciplinary exchange in the creative process.

- Identifying specific individuals, groups, or organizations that share your creative vision and values.

- Exploring the unique skills, knowledge, and resources that each collaborator could bring to the project.

- Developing a more inclusive, participatory, and socially engaged approach to creative production.

Instructions

1. Draw a central point representing your creative collaboration opportunities. Label this "My Creative Collaboration Opportunities."

2. Draw main branches from your central point for different categories of potential collaborators. For example

A. Other artists or creatives in your field

B. Professionals from complementary or contrasting fields

C. Cultural institutions or organizations

D. Community groups or grassroots initiatives

3. Under each main branch, draw twigs for specific individuals, groups, or organizations you would like to collaborate with. For example, this could be a mentor or advisor with wisdom and guidance who would share their creative journey.

4. Draw connecting lines between collaboration opportunities that could be combined, sequenced, or integrated into a larger creative vision or project.

5. Include a branch for brainstorming the specific projects, initiatives, or creative outputs that could emerge from each collaboration, plus the key milestones, resources, or agreements needed to bring the partnership to fruition.

6. Create a separate branch to identify the skills, knowledge, or capacities you need to develop or acquire to be an effective collaborator and creative partner.

7. Review your creative collaboration mind map regularly, using it as a guide for reaching out to potential partners, initiating new projects, and expanding the scope and impact of your creative practice.

Exercise 74: Mind Map Your Creative Solutions to Everyday Challenges

Objective

This mind map helps cultivate a habit of creative problem-solving in your daily life, enhancing your ability to navigate everyday challenges and seize opportunities. You will be:

- Recognizing the pervasiveness of creative opportunities in your daily life and work.

- Identifying specific areas or situations where conventional approaches may be limiting or ineffective.

- Exploring unconventional, imaginative, or innovative solutions to common challenges or tasks.

- Developing a more adaptable, resourceful, and proactive mindset in the face of obstacles or constraints.

Instructions

1. Draw a central point representing your everyday challenges or tasks that could benefit from creative solutions. Label this "Applying Creative Solutions to Everyday Challenges."

2. Draw main branches from your central point for different categories of everyday challenges or tasks, including

A. Personal organization and productivity

B. Interpersonal communication and relationships

C. Health and wellness

D. Financial management and budgeting

E. Home maintenance and improvement

F. Work projects and responsibilities

G. Community engagement and activism

H. Environmental sustainability and conservation

3. Under each main branch, draw twigs for specific challenges, tasks, or situations you encounter in that area of your life, along with the conventional approaches or limitations you want to overcome. For example, you could streamline your morning routine to minimize stress and maximize focus.

4. Draw connecting lines between everyday challenges or tasks that share similar patterns, root causes, or potential synergies.

5. Include a branch for brainstorming specific creative solutions, strategies, or techniques for addressing each everyday challenge or task, drawing from a wide range of fields, for example, applying design thinking or agile methodologies to personal productivity challenges.

6. Create a separate branch to identify the skills, resources, or support systems you need to implement and sustain each creative solution. Map out a plan for acquiring or accessing these enablers over time.

Creating and using these mind maps helps you harness the power of visual thinking, associative reasoning, and creative problem-solving to optimize your performance, expand your horizons, and make a positive impact in your personal and professional life. These tools will help you cultivate the mindsets, strategies, and collaborative relationships that are essential for thriving in an increasingly complex, dynamic, and interconnected world.

Chapter 12

Building Resilience and Enhancing Tenacity

Strength is not about how much you can handle before you break; it's about how much you can handle after you've broken.

Robert Tew

There is a common misconception that men with ADHD lack resilience and the ability to bounce back from setbacks. The idea that ADHD men lack resilience, however, couldn't be further from the truth. Many men with ADHD have developed remarkable resilience and tenacity precisely because of the challenges they've had to navigate throughout their lives.

Living with ADHD often means confronting daily obstacles and difficulties that can be overwhelming and demoralizing. Men with ADHD face a constant barrage of stressors and setbacks that can erode their sense of self-worth and confidence. This can be from struggling to meet societal expectations and conforming to neurotypical norms to managing the practical challenges of organization, time management, and impulsivity.

Applying ADHD Resilience and Tenacity Across All Areas of Life

The resilience and tenacity that men with ADHD develop through their experiences can be a powerful asset in life. They have learned to channel their strengths and apply them to different challenges and opportunities daily.

They learn to build and maintain healthy relationships despite their struggles with emotional regulation and communication. They can do well in the workplace despite struggling with time management, organization, and focus. They can even perform in educational settings that are not designed for the neurodivergent brain.

David Neelman, founder of JetBlue Airways and an open advocate for men with ADHD, has long said that creativity, resilience, and risk tolerance are all primary reasons he is successful. He developed the ability to bounce back from failure *because* of his struggles and is much stronger because of it.

Mind Mapping for Channeling ADHD Resilience and Tenacity

Mind mapping may not help us build resilience, but it can certainly be a powerful tool to help us harness and amplify the tenacity within each of us. When using mind maps, we can:

- Learn to reframe challenges as opportunities for growth and learning.

- Break larger goals down into smaller, more manageable steps that promote the further development of resilience and tenacity.

- Identify areas where we can leverage our strengths and resources to push through challenges and deal with our setbacks in a healthy way.

- Cultivate a growth mindset that fuels our belief in our ability to strengthen our skill sets so that we can continue to stretch ourselves and achieve success in our lives.

Mind Mapping Exercises for Creating a Resilient, Tenacious Life

Exercise 75: Mind Map Your Key Life-Changing Moments

Objective

This mind map helps provide you with a visual representation of the significant events and experiences that have shaped your life to this point. You will be:

- Gaining a clearer understanding of the key factors that have shaped your identity and perspective.

- Recognizing the interconnectedness of different experiences and their cumulative impact on your growth.

- Identifying recurring themes, challenges, or opportunities that have emerged throughout your life.

- Developing greater self-awareness and a deeper appreciation for the unique journey that has brought you to where you are today.

Instructions

1. Draw a central point representing your life journey. Label this "My Key Life-Changing Moments."

2. Draw main branches from your central point for different categories or types of life-changing moments, including

   A. Family and relationships

   B. Education and learning

   C. Career and professional development

   D. Personal growth and self-discovery

   E. Health and well-being

F. Travel and cultural experiences

D. Challenges and adversity

H. Achievements and successes

3. Under each main branch, draw twigs for specific events, experiences, or turning points that stand out as particularly significant or transformative in that area of your life. For example, this could be the birth or loss of a loved one or a pivotal conversation or encounter with a mentor or teacher.

4. For each life-changing moment, include a brief description of what happened, plus any key emotions, insights, or lessons that emerged from the experience.

5. Draw connecting lines between life-changing moments that are related or built upon each other in meaningful ways.

6. Include a branch for reflecting on the overall lessons, insights, or personal growth resulting from these life-changing moments.

7. Review your life-changing moments mind map regularly, using it as a tool for self-reflection, gratitude, and personal growth.

8. Update the map as new significant experiences or insights emerge.

Exercise 76: Mind Map Your Past Success

Objective

This mind map helps cultivate self-awareness and appreciation for your resilience, drawing inspiration and confidence from past successes to face future challenges. You will be:

- Gaining a clearer understanding of the strengths, skills, and strategies that have contributed to your successes.

- Developing a greater sense of self-efficacy and confidence in your ability to overcome obstacles and achieve your goals.

• Identifying patterns or themes in the types of challenges you have successfully navigated in the past.

• Creating a visual reminder of your past triumphs to draw upon for motivation and inspiration in the face of future challenges.

Instructions

1. Draw a central point representing your past triumphs. Label this "My Triumphs."

2. Draw main branches from your central point for different categories or types of triumphs, including

    A. Personal growth and self-discovery

    B. Relationships and social connections

    C. Academic or educational achievements

    D. Career or professional milestones

    E. Creative or artistic accomplishments

    F. Athletic or physical feats

3. Under each main branch, draw twigs for specific examples of triumphs in that category, drawing from the life-changing moments you identified in the previous exercise.

4. For each triumph, include a brief description of what you accomplished and any key factors or strategies that contributed to your success. This can include specific skills, knowledge, or expertise that you developed or applied.

5. Draw connecting lines between triumphs that share similar themes, strategies, or lessons learned.

6. Include a branch for reflecting on the overall lessons, insights, or personal growth that have resulted from these triumphs.

7. Update the map as new triumphs or insights emerge.

Exercise 77: Mind Map Your Key Personality Traits for Resilience

Objective

This mind map helps you identify and explore the key personality traits that contribute to resilience and tenacity in the face of adversity. You will be:

- Gaining a clearer understanding of the personal qualities and characteristics that underlie your resilience.

- Developing a greater sense of self-awareness and appreciation for your strengths and capabilities.

- Identifying patterns or themes in the types of traits that have served you well in navigating challenges and setbacks.

- Cultivating a more empowering and growth-oriented mindset by focusing on your innate resilience and potential.

Instructions

1. Draw a central point representing the concept of resilience. Label this "Key Personality Traits for Resilience."

2. Draw main branches from your central point for different categories or types of personality traits that contribute to resilience, including

   A. Emotional regulation and self-awareness

   B. Cognitive flexibility and problem-solving

   C. Interpersonal skills and social support

   D. Sense of purpose and meaning

   E. Optimism and positive outlook

   F. Self-efficacy and confidence

3. Under each main branch, draw twigs for specific personality traits or characteristics, such as emotional intelligence and empathy.

4. For each personality trait, include a brief description of what it looks like in action and add any specific examples from your life where you have demonstrated that trait.

5. Draw connecting lines between personality traits that are related or that support and reinforce each other.

6. Include a branch for reflecting on the overall lessons, insights, or personal growth that has occurred.

7. Update the map as new insights or examples emerge.

Exercise 78: Mind Map Your Resilience-Building Strategies

Objective

This mind map helps develop a personalized toolkit of resilience-building strategies, equipping yourself with the skills and mindset to navigate challenges and bounce back from setbacks. You will be:

- Identifying specific tools and techniques that can help you cultivate greater resilience and adaptability.

- Exploring a range of approaches and perspectives for building resilience.

- Creating a visual representation of your resilience toolkit, making it easy to reference and apply in the face of challenges.

- Developing a proactive and empowering approach to building resilience.

Instructions

1. Draw a central point representing your resilience-building strategies. Label this "My Resilience-Building Strategies."

2. Draw main branches from your central point for different categories or types of resilience-building strategies, including

    A. Cognitive strategies

    B. Emotional strategies

    C. Behavioral strategies

    D. Interpersonal strategies

    E. Physical strategies

    F. Spiritual strategies

3. Under each main branch, draw twigs for specific strategies or techniques that fall under that category. For example, a cognitive strategy may be breaking down large problems into smaller, more manageable steps or goals.

4. For each strategy or technique, include a brief description of how it works and any specific examples. Using the cognitive strategy example mentioned above, manageable steps or goals can be broken down via the SMART goal technique.

5. Draw connecting lines between related strategies or ones that support and reinforce each other.

6. Include a branch for reflecting on the overall lessons, insights, or personal growth you hope to achieve.

7. Update the map as new strategies or insights emerge.

Exercise 79: Mind Map Your Everyday Incremental Goals

Objective

This mind map helps you set one percent everyday goals that contribute to ongoing personal growth and development. By cultivating a habit of consistent effort, you will be:

• Identifying specific areas of your life where you want to make gradual, sustainable progress over time.

• Breaking down larger, long-term goals into smaller, more manageable daily actions or habits.

• Creating a visual representation of your incremental goals, making it easy to track and celebrate your progress.

• Developing a proactive and empowering approach to personal growth and development, focusing on consistent effort rather than perfection.

Instructions

1. Draw a central point representing your everyday incremental goals. Label this "My 1% Everyday Goals."

2. Draw main branches from your central point for different areas or domains of your life where you want to make incremental improvements, including

    A. Physical health and well-being

    B. Mental and emotional resilience

    C. Relationships and social connections

    D. Career and professional development

    E. Personal growth and self-awareness

    F. Creativity and self-expression

    G. Spirituality and purpose

3. Under each main branch, draw twigs for specific goals or habits you want to cultivate in that area of your life. For example, you could drink an extra glass of water each day or practice a few minutes of mindfulness or deep breathing.

4. For each incremental goal or habit, include a brief description of why it matters to you, as well as any specific benefits or outcomes.

5. Draw connecting lines between incremental goals that are related or that support and reinforce each other.

6. Include a branch for reflecting on the overall vision, values, or aspirations your incremental goals are designed to support.

7. Update the map as you make progress, encounter obstacles, or identify new areas for growth.

Exercise 80: Mind Map Your Plan for Failure

Objective

This mind map helps you create a proactive plan for dealing with failure in a constructive and resilient manner. You will become used to:

- Recognizing that failure is a natural and inevitable part of the learning and growth processes rather than something to be feared or avoided.

- Identifying specific strategies and coping mechanisms for managing the emotional and practical impacts of failure.

- Creating a visual representation of your plan for failure, making it easy to reference and apply in the face of setbacks.

- Developing a proactive and empowering approach to failure, focusing on learning, growth, and resilience rather than self-judgment or blame.

Instructions

1. Draw a central point representing your plan for failure. Label this "My Plan for Failure."

2. Draw main branches from your central point for different aspects or components of your plan for failure, including

A. Emotional regulation and self-care

B. Cognitive reframing and perspective-taking

C. Problem-solving and action-planning

D. Social support and communication

E. Learning and growth mindset

F. Resilience and perseverance

3. Under each main branch, draw twigs for specific strategies or techniques that you can use to navigate failure in that area. For example, practicing self-compassion and kindness toward yourself in the face of setbacks.

4. For each strategy or technique, include a brief description of how it can help you navigate failure, plus any specific examples or applications. For example, self-compassion can consist of speaking to yourself as you would to your best friend or being curious about a mistake made.

5. Draw connecting lines between related strategies or ones that support and reinforce each other.

6. Include a branch for reflecting on the overall lessons, insights, or personal growth you hope to achieve through your proactive plan for failure.

7. Update the map as new strategies or insights emerge.

Exercise 81: Mind Map Your Resilience Goals

Objective

This mind map helps you strengthen your resilience by setting concrete goals and action plans focused on building resilience skills and mindsets. You will be:

• Identifying specific areas or skills related to resilience that you want to develop or enhance.

• Creating a clear and compelling vision of what greater resilience looks and feels like for you.

• Breaking down larger resilience goals into smaller, more manageable steps or milestones.

• Developing a proactive and intentional approach to building resilience rather than simply reacting to adversity when it arises.

Instructions

1. Draw a central point representing your resilience goals. Label this "My Resilience Goals."

2. Draw main branches from your central point for different areas or aspects of resilience that you want to focus on in your goals, including

    A. Emotional regulation and self-awareness

    B. Cognitive flexibility and realistic optimism

    C. Social connection and support

    D. Sense of purpose and meaning

    E. Physical health and well-being

    F. Problem-solving and resourcefulness

3. Under each main branch, draw twigs for specific goals you want to set in that area of resilience, focusing on measurable, actionable, and time-bound objectives.

4. For each resilience goal, include a brief explanation of why it matters to you, plus any specific benefits or outcomes you hope to achieve through pursuing that goal.

5. Draw connecting lines between related goals or ones that support and reinforce each other.

6. Include a branch for reflecting on the overall vision, values, or aspirations that your resilience goals are designed to support.

7. Review your resilience goals mind map regularly, using it as a source of motivation, accountability, and celebration.

Exercise 82: Mind Map Your Resilience-Building Habits

Objective

This mind map helps you cultivate resilience as a lifestyle by integrating resilience-building habits into your daily routine. You will be:

- Recognizing the power of small, consistent actions in building resilience over time.

- Identifying specific habits or routines that can support your physical, mental, and emotional well-being.

- Creating a visual representation of your resilience-building habits, making it easy to reference and implement them in your daily life.

- Developing a holistic and integrated approach to resilience rather than relying on isolated strategies or techniques.

- Cultivating a sense of agency and empowerment in your ability to shape your daily experiences and responses to adversity.

Instructions

1. Draw a central point representing your resilience-building habits. Label this "My Resilience-Building Habits."

2. Draw main branches from your central point for different categories or areas of well-being that your habits can support, including

A. Physical well-being

B. Mental and cognitive well-being

C. Emotional well-being

D. Social and relational well-being

E. Spiritual or existential well-being

F. Environmental or contextual well-being

3. Under each main branch, draw twigs for specific habits or routines you want to cultivate in that area of well-being. For example, practicing gratitude by naming three things you're thankful for each evening.

4. For each resilience-building habit, include a brief description of how it can support your well-being and resilience.

5. Draw connecting lines between related habits or ones that support and reinforce each other.

6. Include a branch for reflecting on the overall vision, values, or aspirations your resilience-building habits are designed to support.

7. Update the map as you experiment with new habits, encounter obstacles, or identify new areas for growth.

Exercise 83: Mind Map Your Healthy Celebration Behaviors

Objective

This mind map helps you develop healthy celebration behaviors that promote well-being, fulfillment, and continued growth. You will be:

- Recognizing the importance of celebrating your achievements and milestones healthily and sustainably.

- Identifying specific celebration behaviors or habits that nourish and energize you, while aligning with your values, preferences, and long-term goals.

- Developing a proactive and intentional approach to celebration rather than simply reacting to external validation or expectations.

- Cultivating a sense of joy, gratitude, and self-compassion in your celebrations, rather than self-judgment or comparison.

Instructions

1. Draw a central point representing your approach to celebration. Label this "My Healthy Celebration Behaviors."

2. Draw main branches from your central point for different aspects of healthy celebration, including:

   A. Self-care and nourishment

   B. Gratitude and appreciation

   C. Social connection and support

   D. Personal growth and learning

   E. Contribution and generosity

   F. Rest and rejuvenation

3. Under each main branch, draw twigs for specific celebration behaviors or habits you want to cultivate, such as treating yourself to your favorite meal.

4. For each celebration behavior or habit, include a brief explanation of why it matters to you.

5. Draw connecting lines between celebration behaviors that are related or that support and reinforce each other.

6. Include a branch for reflecting on the overall vision, values, or aspirations that your healthy celebration behaviors are designed to support.

7. Update the map as you experiment with new celebration practices, encounter challenges or setbacks, or identify new areas for growth.

Engaging in mind mapping exercises specifically designed to help you build upon your inherent resilience and tenacity is incredibly empowering. You can not only refocus these characteristics to set and achieve new goals but also develop healthy ways to celebrate good behaviors. This reduces the need to take unhealthy risks as it taps into your brain's reward systems to promote good habit formation and leads to overall life satisfaction.

Conclusion

As men with ADHD, we certainly encounter a unique set of challenges throughout our lives, but we are also presented with opportunities that are unique to us because of our incredible neurodivergent way of thinking. We need to remember that our experiences and ADHD do not define us. By using the strategies, tools, and techniques available to us, we can harness our full potential and create a life of purpose, fulfillment, and success.

Mind mapping is a visual and dynamic tool for organizing information, generating ideas, and solving problems in a way that aligns with the strengths and preferences of the ADHD brain. Embracing this technique and making it a regular part of our personal and professional lives helps us unlock new levels of clarity, creativity, and productivity.

However, the benefits of mind mapping go far beyond practical applications. When we tap into our unique set of strengths, like divergent thinking, hyperfocus, and emotional sensitivity, men with ADHD can achieve remarkable things in all areas of life. This means you *do* have the ability to build deeper, more authentic relationships, excel in your chosen careers, and make meaningful contributions to the world around you.

A lot of the challenges you will have come from inside—from a belief that something is wrong with you. So, before you close this book, I want you to know that you are not broken, and there is *nothing* wrong with you. You have everything you need to create the life you want. Your unique brain wiring is not a limitation but a gift—one that can be harnessed and celebrated through the power of mind mapping and a commitment to personal growth.

Keep exploring, keep learning, and keep mapping your way to a brighter, more fulfilling future. The world needs your creativity, passion, and unparalleled ability to think differently and solve problems in innovative ways. Embrace your ADHD superpowers, and let them guide you to success in your life.

THANK YOU

Thank you for purchasing my book.

I would like to ask you for a small favor. **Could you please leave a review on the platform? Leaving a review is the best way to support me as an independent author.**

Your feedback is valuable to me. It helps me write books that are aligned with your desired outcomes. I would greatly appreciate hearing from you.

You can scan the QR code to leave a review.

US   UK   CAD

Do not forget to download your THREE bonuses for free!!

https://selftransformationpath.com/BundlePB

You can also scan this QR code to get access.

If you are looking to explore self-help and personal growth, I invite you to discover my books on Amazon. They offer many tips and strategies to support your journey.

References

Achoru, F. (2022, October 7). *Richard Branson's simple habit that could help you boom with ideas.* Medium. https://medium.com/illumination/richard-bransons-simple-habit-that-could-help-you-boom-with-ideas-

Arjen. (2020, August 27). *How to clear your mind using mind maps.* MindMaps Unleashed. https://mindmapsunleashed.com/clear-your-mind

Beck, C. (2022, November 14). *Drawing mind maps.* The OT Toolbox. https://www.theottoolbox.com/drawing-mind-maps/

Beckwith, A., & Parkhurst, E. (2022, July 1). *The mental health benefits of decluttering.* Extension.USU. https://extension.usu.edu/mentalhealth/articles/the-mental-benefits-of-decluttering

Belsky, G. (2023). *Executive functioning: What is executive function?* understood.org. https://www.understood.org/en/articles/what-is-executive-function

Brusegar, C. (2021, February 4). *Using mind mapping to declutter your brain.* The Best Is yet to Come. https://carolbrusegar.com/using-mind-mapping-to-declutter-your-brain/

Cai, I. (2022, May 5). *3 ways to use mind mapping to design your career & get unstuck.* Career Relaunch. https://medium.com/career-relaunch/3-ways-of-using-mind-mapping-to-design-your-career-get-unstuck-6fea5e492348

Cooper, R. K., & Sawaf, A. (1998). *Executive EQ: emotional intelligence in leadership and organizations.* Perigee Books.

Emily. (n.d.). *How I'm learning to manage rejection-sensitive dysphoria.* Authentically Emily. https://www.authenticallyemily.uk/blog/how-im-learning-to-manage-rejection-sensitive-dysphoria#google_vignette

Gjorgievska, K. (2018, September 13). *How to make a financial plan with a mind map.* IMindQ. https://www.imindq.com/inspiration/how-to-make-a-financial-plan-with-a-mind-map/

Hackney, & Jones. (2022). *Stop Anxious Thoughts Now: Untangle your mind and eliminate worries. Easy techniques that reduce overthinking and prevent panic attacks and anxiety.* Barnes and Noble.

Hardy, J. (n.d.). *Mind mapping: A powerful tool for planning novels.* Pinterest. https://br.pinterest.com/pin/342766221641057208/

Hinkley, M. P. (n.d.). *Marjorie Pay Hinckley quotes.* Goodreads. https://www.goodreads.com/author/quotes/226482.Marjorie_Pay_Hinckley

Hoffman, H. (n.d.). *Hans Hofmann quotes.* Goodreads. https://www.goodreads.com/author/quotes/5729.Hans_Hofmann

Holmes, O. W. (n.d.). Oliver Wendell Holmes quotes. BrainyQuote. https://www.brainyquote.com/authors/oliver-wendell-holmes-sr-quotes

How to use mind maps to organize your life. (2017, January 24). Heartwork Organizing. https://heartworkorg.com/2017/01/24/you-use-mindmaps-to-organize/

Hubbard, E. (n.d.). *Elbert Hubbard quotes.* Goodreads. https://www.goodreads.com/author/quotes/114059.Elbert_Hubbard

References

Hutchins, C. (2015, October 14). *Mind mapping - get the clutter out of your head!* Do a New Thing. https://doanewthing.com/mind-mapping/

Ingram, H. (n.d.). *Effortless thought organization: Mastering mind mapping techniques.* Work Play Refresh. https://www.workplayrefresh.com/blog/organize-your-thoughts-with-mind-mapping

James, W. (n.d.). *William James quotes.* Goodreads. https://www.goodreads.com/author/quotes/15865.William_James

Kajka, N., & Kulik, A. (2021). The influence of metacognitive strategies on the improvement of reaction inhibition processes in children with ADHD. *International Journal of Environmental Research and Public Health, 18*(3), 878. https://doi.org/10.3390/ijerph18030878

Klein, A. (2021, May 20). *Adult ADHD symptoms and signs.* Psych Central. https://psychcentral.com/adhd/adult-adhd-symptoms

Lanzetta, M. (2023, May 21). *Memory, mind maps, and meta-prompts.* LinkedIn. https://www.linkedin.com/pulse/memory-mind-maps-meta-prompts-mike-lanzetta

Leisman, G., & Melillo, R. (2022). Front and center: Maturational dysregulation of frontal lobe functional neuroanatomic connections in attention deficit hyperactivity disorder. *Frontiers in Neuroanatomy, 16.* https://doi.org/10.3389/fnana.2022.936025

Ltd, X. (n.d.-a). *6 ways to stop overthinking everything.* Xmind. https://xmind.app/embed/HuHj/

Ltd, X. (n.d.-b). *How to manage your time with mind mapping (hint: you don't always need to).* Xmind. https://xmind.app/blog/mind-map-time-management/

Mapping my way to mental clarity. (2017, August 14). LucidChart. https://www.lucidchart.com/blog/mapping-my-way-to-mental-clarity

Mareva, S., The CALM Team, & Holmes, J. (2023, June 13). *Mapping neurodevelopmental diversity in executive function.* medrxiv.org. https://www.medrxiv.org/content/medrxiv/early/2023/06/16/2023.06.15.23291392.full.pdf

Munger, C. T. (n.d.). *Charles T. Munger quotes.* Goodreads. https://www.goodreads.com/author/quotes/236437.Charles_T_Munger

Peters, T. (n.d.). *Top 10 Tom Peters quotes.* BrainyQuote. https://www.brainyquote.com/lists/authors/top-10-tom-peters-quotes

Plutarch. (n.d.). *Plutarch quotes.* BrainyQuote. https://www.brainyquote.com/quotes/plutarch_161334

Postmedia. (2020, May 2). *Five reasons why mind mapping helps with career development.* Financial Post. https://financialpost.com/personal-finance/taxes/five-reasons-why-mind-mapping-helps-with-career-development

Quinn, P. O. (2014, October 13). *Attention-deficit/hyperactivity disorder (ADHD).* National Institute of Mental Health (NIMH). https://www.nimh.nih.gov/health/statistics/attention-deficit-hyperactivity-disorder-adhd#:~:text=The%20overall%20prevalence%20of%20current

Ryun, J. (n.d.). *Jim Ryun quotes.* Goodreads. https://www.goodreads.com/quotes/172268-motivation-is-what-gets-you-started-habit-is-what-keeps

Schwarzenegger, A. (n.d.). *Arnold Schwarzenegger quotes.* Goodreads. https://www.goodreads.com/author/quotes/67084.Arnold_Schwarzenegger

Sedgwick-Müller, J. A., Müller-Sedgwick, U., Adamou, M., Catani, M., Champ, R., Gudjónsson, G., Hank, D., Pitts, M., Young, S., & Asherson, P. (2022). University students with attention deficit hyperactivity disorder (ADHD): A consensus statement from the UK Adult ADHD Network (UKAAN). *BMC Psychiatry, 22*(1). https://doi.org/10.1186/s12888-022-03898-z

Sippl, A. (2024, January 16). *Mind mapping: How to help your teen learn to plan ahead.* Life Skills Advocate. https://lifeskillsadvocate.com/blog/mind-mapping-how-to-help-your-teen-learn-to-plan-ahead/

Stibbe, T., Huang, J., Paucke, M., Ulke, C., & Strauss, M. (2020). Gender differences in adult ADHD: Cognitive function assessed by the test of attentional performance. *PLOS ONE, 15*(10), e0240810. https://doi.org/10.1371/journal.pone.0240810

Stop overthinking and start doing: Overcoming analysis paralysis. (n.d.). Creately. https://creately.com/guides/overcoming-analysis-paralysis/

10 executive functioning skills: The ultimate guide. (n.d.). The Pathway 2 Success. https://www.thepathway2success.com/10-executive-functioning-skills-the-ultimate-guide/

Tew, R. (n.d.). *Robert Tew quotes.* Goodreads. https://www.goodreads.com/author/quotes/13848712.Robert_Tew#:~:text=Robert%20Tew%20Quotes&text=Respect%20your-self%20enough%20to%20walk

Theophrastus. (n.d.). *Theophrastus quotes.* Goodreads. https://www.goodreads.com/author/quotes/185668.Theophrastus

Tredgold, G. (2016, August 4). *55 inspiring quotes that show the power of emotional intelligence.* Inc.com. https://www.inc.com/gordon-tredgold/55-inspiring-quotes-that-show-the-importance-of-emotional-intelligence.html

Tsunetomo, Y. (n.d.). *Yamamoto Tsunetomo quotes.* Goodreads. https://www.goodreads.com/author/quotes/14204578.Yamamoto_Tsunetomo?page=2

Understanding rejection sensitive dysphoria (RSD) & ADHD. (n.d.). Frida. https://www.talkwithfrida.com/learn/rejection-sensitive-dysphoria/

What Your Conflict Resolution Style Says About You and Is It Healthy? (2023, May 26). https://www.verywellmind.com/5-conflict-resolution-styles-is-yours-healthy-7503353#toc-the-five-conflict-resolution-styles

Z, S. (2017, January 3). *How to use mind mapping to manage your career.* LinkedIn. https://www.linkedin.com/pulse/how-use-mind-mapping-manage-your-career-simon-zhu

Mind Map Example References

Activity 1.3 mind map. (n.d.). Mindomo. https://www.mindomo.com/mindmap/activity-13-mind-map-197b318c8bf74a64b677b2ea34299dd1

Biggerplate. (n.d.). *Financial planning.* Pinterest. https://www.pinterest.com/pin/694117361290343064/

Career plan mind map template. (n.d.). Venngage. https://venngage.com/templates/mind-maps/career-plan-mind-map-565d5aa8-63d1-4feb-9bd8-4acbc83e2062

Casseday, L. (n.d.). *150 mind map ideas.* Pinterest. https://www.pinterest.com/lcasseday/mind-maps/

Complete mind map of feelings-rejection-sensitive. (n.d.). E Draw Mind. https://www.edrawmind.com/mind-maps/26798/complete-mind-map-of-feelings

Corkin, P. (n.d.). *Financial planning and management.* MindMeister. https://www.mindmeister.com/54432995/financial-planning-and-management

References

Financial planning mind map. (n.d.). Visual-Paradigm. https://online.visual-paradigm.com/diagrams/templates/mind-map-diagram/financial-planning-mind-map/

House organizing mind map. (n.d.). Edrawsoft. https://www.edrawsoft.com/template-house-organizing-mind-map.html

Indeed Editorial Team. (2022, October 1). *Effective mind mapping examples to help build your career.* Indeed Australia. https://au.indeed.com/career-advice/career-development/mind-map-examples

Mind maps: Figuring out household chores. (2010, March 11) 5 Minute Mom. https://5minutemom.blogspot.com/2010/03/mind-maps-figuring-out-household-chores.html

Mind map for relationship building. (n.d.). Visual Paradigm. https://online.visual-paradigm.com/diagrams/templates/mind-map-diagram/mind-map-for-relationship-building-/

Mind map your financial plan. (2016). Using Mind Maps. https://www.usingmindmaps.com/mind-map-financial-plan.html

Mood journal mind map to regulate emotions behavior patterns. (n.d.). This Human Feeling. https://www.thisfeelinghuman.com/mind-map-of-feelings#:~:text=Mind%20mapping%20is%20a%20quick

Psychological well-being. (n.d.). Mindomo. https://www.mindomo.com/mindmap/psychological-well-being-44990ca4e88cc645454270c61447ec22

Relationship mind map. (n.d.). Visual-Paradigm. https://online.visual-paradigm.com/diagrams/templates/mind-map-diagram/relationship-mind-map-/

Roller Kiddie. (n.d.). *Mind map emotion.* Teachers Pay Teachers. https://www.teacherspayteachers.com/browse?search=mind%20map%20emotion

Saul-Paterson, J. (n.d.). *How to create a career mind map.* Stay Nimble. https://staynimble.co.uk/blog/advancing-your-career-with-a-mind-map/

Time management mind map: Improve productivity effectively. (n.d.). Edrawsoft. https://www.edrawmind.com/article/time-management-mind-map.htm

Glossary

Cognitive distortions:

Cognitive distortions are inaccurate and irrational thoughts that influence our emotions and behaviors. These are patterns of thinking that are often negative and unrealistic, such as thinking in black-and-white terms, overgeneralizing, or catastrophizing (expecting the worst).

SMART goals:

SMART goals are ones that are Specific, Measurable, Achievable, Relevant, and Time-bound. This method helps to set clear and reachable goals by defining exactly what you want to achieve, how you'll measure your progress, ensuring the goal is realistic, making sure it matters to you, and setting a deadline.

Active Listening:

Active listening is more than just hearing what someone says to you. It is a process whereby you show someone you are listening through appropriate eye contact and verbal and nonverbal communication. It also involves using open questions, summarizing and paraphrasing to check understanding, and being nonjudgmental. The focus is on the other person—rather than thinking about a response, you are being mindful and fully concentrating on listening to their message.

Conflict Response Styles:

The Thomas-Kilmann Conflict Mode Instrument (TKI) is one of the most widely-used models of conflict management. It identifies five conflict resolution styles that range across a spectrum of assertiveness and cooperation with others. They are competing, avoiding, collaborating, accommodating, and compromising. For more information on each of the conflict resolution styles, see the references list.

"I" statements:

A way of expressing your feelings and needs without blaming or criticizing others. It typically starts with "I feel" or "I need" and is followed by a description of the situation and its impact on you. For example, "I feel upset when the house is messy because it makes it hard for me to relax."

Pomodoro technique:

A time management method that involves breaking work into intervals, usually 25 minutes long, separated by short breaks. After four intervals, take a longer break. This technique helps improve focus and productivity by encouraging regular breaks and maintaining concentration.